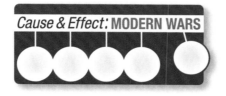

Cause & Effect:
The War on Terror

Don Nardo

San Diego, CA

© 2018 ReferencePoint Press, Inc.
Printed in the United States

For more information, contact:
ReferencePoint Press, Inc.
PO Box 27779
San Diego, CA 92198
www.ReferencePointPress.com

LIBRARY OF CONGRESS CATALOGING-IN-PUBLICATION DATA

Name: Nardo, Don, 1947– author.
Title: Cause & Effect : The War on Terror/by Don Nardo.
Other titles: Cause and Effect, the War on Terror
Description: San Diego, CA: ReferencePoint Press, Inc., 2018. | Series:
    Cause & Effect | Includes bibliographical references and index.
Identifiers: LCCN 2017009892 (print) | LCCN 2017016038 (ebook) | ISBN
    9781682821718 (eBook) | ISBN 9781682821701 (hardback)
Subjects: LCSH: War on Terrorism, 2001–2009—Juvenile literature. |
    Terrorism—United States—Prevention—Juvenile literature. |
    Terrorism—Prevention—Juvenile literature. | Terrorism—History--21st
    century—Juvenile literature
Classification: LCC HV6432 (ebook) | LCC HV6432 .N369 2018 (print) | DDC
    363.3250973--dc23
LC record available at https://lccn.loc.gov/2017009892

CONTENTS

"History is a complex study of the many causes that have influenced happenings of the past and the complicated effects of those varied causes."

—William & Mary School of Education,
Center for Gifted Education

U nderstanding the causes and effects of historical events, including those that occur within the context of war, is rarely simple. The Cold War's Cuban Missile Crisis, for instance, resulted from a complicated—and at times convoluted—series of events set in motion by US, Soviet, and Cuban actions. And that crisis, in turn, shaped interactions between the United States and the former Soviet Union for years to come. Had any of these events not taken place or had they occurred under different circumstances, the effects might have been something else altogether.

The value of analyzing cause and effect in the context of modern wars, therefore, is not necessarily to identify a single cause for a singular event. The real value lies in gaining a greater understanding of history as a whole and being able to recognize the many factors that give shape and direction to historic events. As outlined by the National Center for History in the Schools at the University of California–Los Angeles, these factors include "the importance of the individual in history . . . the influence of ideas, human interests, and beliefs; and . . . the role of chance, the accidental and the irrational."

ReferencePoint's Cause & Effect: Modern Wars series examines wars of the modern age by focusing on specific causes and consequences. For instance, in *Cause & Effect (Modern Wars): The Cold War*, a chapter explores whether the US military buildup in the 1980s helped end the Cold War. And in *Cause & Effect (Modern Wars): The Vietnam War*, one chapter delves into this question: "How Did Fear of Communism Lead to US Intervention in Vietnam?" Every book in the series includes thoughtful discussion of questions like these—supported by facts, examples, and a mix of fully documented primary and secondary source quotes. Each title also includes an overview of the event so that readers have a broad context for understanding the more detailed discussions of specific causes and their effects.

The value of such study is not limited to the classroom; it can also be applied to many areas of contemporary life. The ability to analyze and interpret history's causes and consequences is a form of critical thinking. Critical thinking is crucial in many professions, ranging from law enforcement to science. Critical thinking is also essential for developing an educated citizenry that fully understands the rights and obligations of living in a free society. The ability to sift through and analyze complex processes and events and identify their possible outcomes enables people in that society to make important decisions.

The Cause & Effect: Modern Wars series has two primary goals. One is to help students think more critically about history and develop a true understanding of its complexities. The other is to help build a foundation for those students to become fully participating members of the society in which they live.

IMPORTANT EVENTS OF THE WAR ON TERROR

2003
US military forces invade Iraq and remove dictator Saddam Hussein from power.

2002
A terrorist group with links to al Qaeda bombs a nightclub in Bali, Indonesia, killing twenty people.

1979
The Soviet Union invades Afghanistan, setting in motion events that will lead to the formation of the terrorist group al Qaeda.

1998
Al Qaeda operatives bomb the US embassies in Tanzania and Kenya.

1980   1985   1990   1995   2000   2005

1988
Saudi political activist Osama bin Laden establishes al Qaeda.

2001
On September 11, nineteen al Qaeda operatives hijack four US airliners, crashing three of them into buildings in New York City and Washington, DC. The fourth crashes into a field in Pennsylvania. On September 14, Congress authorizes the use of force against those held responsible for the terrorist attacks, thereby launching the War on Terror. On October 7, the United States and its allies invade Afghanistan.

6

2009
An American army officer kills thirteen people at Fort Hood, Texas, to demonstrate his opposition to US operations in Afghanistan.

2010
An estimated 13,200 people are killed by terrorists worldwide.

2013
President Barack Obama announces that the War on Terror will henceforth be known as Overseas Contingency Operations.

2011
A team of US Navy SEALs enters Pakistan and kills al Qaeda leader Osama bin Laden; a US missile fired from a drone kills American-born terrorist Anwar al-Awlaki in Yemen.

2010   2011   2012   2013   2014   2015

2014
The terrorist group known as the Islamic State of Iraq and Syria (ISIS) proclaims the formation of an Islamic caliphate with the goal of eventually controlling the world.

2015
The ISIS-inspired terrorist group Boko Haram kills 7,512 people in Nigeria.

2016
ISIS leader Abu Yasser calls on millions of Muslims to rise up against Western countries.

Not the First American War on Terror

A merica's launch of the so-called War on Terror late in 2001 was a clear-cut example of historical cause and effect. The cause in this case was the momentous event often called September 11 or 9/11 for short. On September 11, 2001, members of the terrorist group al Qaeda crashed hijacked passenger airplanes into New York City's World Trade Center and the Pentagon in Washington, DC. Close to three thousand people died that day.

The effect of these attacks was the launch of the War on Terror by US president George W. Bush. Speaking to a joint session of Congress on September 20, Bush said, "Tonight we are a country awakened to danger and called to defend freedom. Our grief has turned to anger, and anger to resolution. Whether we bring our enemies to justice, or bring justice to our enemies, justice will be done." He added, "Our war on terror begins with al Qaeda, but it does not end there. It will not end until every terrorist group of global reach has been found, stopped and defeated."[1]

> "Tonight we are a country awakened to danger and called to defend freedom."[1]
>
> —President George W. Bush

A History of Trying to Avoid Foreign Wars

The vast majority of Americans and foreigners listening to Bush's words that evening agreed that al Qaeda and groups like it needed to be brought to justice. What most of them did not realize at the time was that the proposed war against terrorist groups was not America's first war on terror. Terrorism and US military efforts to battle it date back almost to the country's founding in the late 1700s.

The terrorists of that earlier time were the Barbary pirates, a large group of thugs and thieves based in Algiers, Tripoli, and other small North African states. (These were not full-fledged nations. Tripoli, for example, was then a province of the Ottoman Empire, centered in Turkey.)

American troubles with these pirates began after the nation achieved independence from Great Britain in 1783. Preceding the American Revolution, the American colonists had the protection of Great Britain's Royal Navy, then the world's largest nautical military force. After 1783, however, the British, not surprisingly, withdrew that defensive shield. Only two years later, the ruler of Algiers declared war on the United States, seized several of its ships, and demanded hefty ransoms for their return. At the time, the cash-strapped American government lacked the funds needed to build a navy strong enough to deal with this early form of terrorism.

Al Qaeda's attacks on the World Trade Center in 2001 prompted the US government to institute security strategies to prevent future disasters and seek out those responsible. The resulting War on Terror has since broadened to target not only terror groups but also nations that harbor them.

That situation potentially changed in 1794 when Congress authorized the building of the first six warships of the US Navy. However, for a variety of reasons, the first two American presidents, George Washington and John Adams, did not see fit to use those vessels against the Barbary pirates. One of those reasons was a viewpoint that their colleague Thomas Jefferson later put into words:

> Determined as we are to avoid, if possible, wasting the energies of our people in war and destruction, we shall avoid implicating ourselves with powers [overseas], even in support of principles which we mean to pursue. They have so many other interests different from ours, that we must avoid being entangled in them. We believe we can enforce these principles as to ourselves by peaceable means.[2]

Shock Waves Across the World

Upon gaining the presidency in 1801, Jefferson had every intention of upholding the policy of avoiding foreign entanglements. But the continued threat of piracy forced him to do otherwise. Not long after his first inauguration in 1801, the Barbary state of Tripoli demanded heavy ransom payments from the US government. When Jefferson refused to pay, Tripoli's ruler declared war on the United States. Thereafter, Barbary naval forces increased their capture and enslavement of US sailors and demanded still more ransom payments.

During one of these attempts to terrorize and squeeze money from the United States, the brigands captured the USS *Philadelphia* and its crew. Jefferson responded by sending a squadron of US warships to the Mediterranean to protect American merchant vessels from the pirates. In the summer of 1804 he ordered the USS *Constitution* and other warships to open fire on port installations in Tripoli. This barrage inflicted heavy damage on the enemy.

The climax of Jefferson's war on terror, however, was a land battle. Catching the pirates and their supporters by surprise, early in 1805 a small force of US Marines commanded by William Eaton assaulted

Derna, Tripoli's second-largest city. After a few weeks the city surrendered and soon afterward the Barbary states sued for peace.

This series of events sent shock waves across Europe and the rest of the world. Emboldened European leaders swiftly made it known that they too would refuse to pay the pirates' ransoms and would instead authorize military strikes on them. The result was that, as University of Virginia scholar Robert F. Turner puts it, "centuries of terror on the high seas soon came to an end."[3]

Peace Through Strength

A number of modern scholars have pointed out similarities between Jefferson's clash with the Barbary pirates and the modern War on Terror. Before 9/11, Turner writes, "neither the United States nor its European allies were willing to seriously confront international terrorists." The result was that the terrorists "had little reason to fear any serious consequences." The shock of the 9/11 attacks instantly changed the situation, Turner continues, by inducing the United States and its allies to actively oppose terrorists.

> "Today's terrorists, like the pirates of yore, are widely recognized to be the common enemies of all mankind."[4]
>
> —University of Virginia scholar Robert F. Turner

Today's terrorists, like the pirates of yore, are widely recognized to be the common enemies of all mankind. Jefferson was correct in observing that "an insult unpunished becomes the parent of many others." There is much wisdom to be learned from his successful campaign to bring an end to state sponsored terrorism on the high seas two centuries ago.[4]

CHAPTER ONE

A Brief History of the War on Terror

The War on Terror, sometimes referred to as the Global War on Terrorism, was an international conflict set in motion by the September 11, 2001, attacks on New York City and Washington, DC. US president George W. Bush used the phrase a few days after the terrorist organization al Qaeda committed those assaults. In the decade that followed, officials and the news media used *War on Terror* as a general catchall term. It included a wide range of military, political, legal, and other tactics directed at groups and/or individuals who had committed violent acts against the United States and its allies.

A Never-Ending Undertaking?

During those same years, a number of American and other Western critics expressed the opinion that the word *terror* was too broad in this context. Terror is a concept, they said, an approach used by certain violent individuals to scare or damage those with whom they disagree. The problem, they reasoned, is that terrorists of one type or another are likely to exist far into the future, possibly even forever. Therefore, waging a full-scale war on the idea of terrorism could well be a never-ending undertaking.

Employing that reasoning, in May 2013 President Barack Obama called into question the use of the term *War on Terror*. "With a decade of experience now to draw from, this is the moment to ask ourselves hard questions about the nature of today's threats and how we should confront them," he stated.

> For all the focus on the use of force, force alone cannot make us safe. We cannot use force everywhere that a radical ideology takes root; and in the absence of a strategy that re-

duces the wellspring of extremism, a perpetual war—through drones or Special Forces or troop deployments—will prove self-defeating, and alter our country in troubling ways.[5]

This speech signaled a new strategy in which the United States would no longer pursue a military effort officially or formally labeled the War on Terror. Since then it has been referred to in antiterrorism circles as the Overseas Contingency Operations. Under that name, the country and its principal allies have continued the battle against violent extremists. But they are targeting and eradicating particular terrorist groups or individuals who pose threats rather than fighting an eternal war against an idea. Thus, struggles against specific terrorists continue as the threats they pose arise. But the more open-ended War on Terror declared by President Bush in 2001 concluded in 2013.

> "Force alone cannot make us safe. We cannot use force everywhere that a radical ideology takes root."[5]
>
> —President Barack Obama

Al Qaeda's Formation

The War on Terror began as a reaction to the 9/11 attacks that killed almost three thousand people. Though the War on Terror began suddenly, the attacks themselves did not. Rather, the perpetrator of 9/11, al Qaeda, headed by Osama bin Laden, put years of careful thought and planning into the operation. The true story of the War on Terror therefore begins years before the first shots were fired.

The chief instigator of the 9/11 attacks, Bin Laden, founded al Qaeda in 1988. A member of a wealthy Saudi family, he had earlier traveled to Afghanistan to fight the Soviets, who had invaded that nation in 1979. Neighboring Pakistan, supported by the United States, wanted to aid the struggling Afghans to push the Soviets out of Afghanistan. To that end, Pakistan and the United States supplied money to fund a contingent of Arabs and other Muslims who created an anti-Soviet resistance movement. They called themselves the mujahideen. Bin Laden rapidly rose to become one of the group's leaders.

The mastermind behind the 9/11 attacks was Osama bin Laden, a Saudi national who helped Muslim resistance groups fight off the Soviet invasion of Afghanistan in 1979. Bin Laden strongly believed Muslim land should not be violated by any uninvited foreign presence.

Later, in 1988, Bin Laden and some of his close followers formed a subgroup that broke away from the mujahideen. The new organization adopted the name al Qaeda, meaning "the Foundation" in Arabic. This was one year before the Soviets, who had suffered heavy casualties in the conflict, withdrew from Afghanistan. Having so recently formed their new group, Bin Laden and his associates felt they should continue fighting, this time for any fellow Muslims who felt they were oppressed in some way.

A Hatred for the West

In Bin Laden's view, just such a situation presented itself soon afterward. In 1991 the United States sent troops to Iraq in order to force Iraqi dictator Saddam Hussein out of the tiny neighboring nation of

Kuwait, which he had recently invaded. Bin Laden and other members of al Qaeda despised Saddam Hussein and wanted him to vacate Kuwait. However, they were strongly against US soldiers using Saudi lands to launch their assaults on Iraq. As non-Muslims, Bin Laden declared, their presence disrespected Arabia's soil, which was sacred to all Muslims. He said at one point,

> For over seven years the United States has been occupying the lands of Islam in the holiest of places, the Arabian Peninsula, plundering its riches, dictating to its rulers, humiliating its people, terrorizing its neighbors, and turning its bases in the Peninsula into a spearhead through which to fight the neighboring Muslim peoples. If some people have in the past argued about the fact of the occupation, all the people of the Peninsula have now acknowledged it. The best proof of this is the Americans' continuing aggression against the Iraqi people using the Peninsula as a staging post.[6]

Bin Laden made it clear that he opposed the Saudi leaders' policy of aiding the United States in its fight with Saddam Hussein. In response, the Saudi leaders revoked his citizenship and kicked him out of the country. This series of events instilled in Bin Laden a bitter hatred for the United States and other Western countries as well as for the Saudi government. Consequently, al Qaeda spokesmen began condemning those nations, often accusing them of crimes they never committed.

To vent their ill will against the United States and its allies, al Qaeda's members eventually started launching terrorist attacks on those countries and their installations around the globe. In August 1998, for instance, Bin Laden ordered the bombing of the US embassies in the African countries of Tanzania and Kenya. The blasts killed more than 220 people and injured some 4,000 more. Al Qaeda agents and sympathizers also blew a huge hole in the side of an American ship,

"For over seven years the United States has been occupying the lands of Islam in the holiest of places, the Arabian Peninsula, plundering its riches."[6]

—Al Qaeda founder Osama bin Laden

the USS *Cole*, which lay at anchor in Yemen, located in the southern sector of the Arabian Peninsula. Seventeen American sailors were killed in the 2000 attack.

Defining the War on Terror

These deeds gave al Qaeda a reputation around the world as a dangerous terrorist organization. But most Americans looked at such assaults as faraway events that did not affect, and certainly did not threaten, their way of life. The United States was not prepared, therefore, for the enormity of al Qaeda's next attack, which proved epic in scope. After three years of secret planning, the group unleashed the nineteen hijackers who crashed planes into the World Trade Center towers and the Pentagon on September 11, 2001.

These dramatic events shocked both Americans and people around the globe. Not since the Japanese attack on Hawaii's Pearl Harbor in 1941 had the United States suffered a major attack on its own soil. As had occurred after the Pearl Harbor tragedy, on September 11 and in the days that followed Americans of all walks of life and political views closed ranks in a display of patriotic solidarity. This nationalistic mood was reflected in the halls of Congress as well. On September 14, the House of Representatives and the Senate passed a joint resolution authorizing the president to use military force against the terrorists responsible for the attacks.

> "The Taliban must act, and act immediately. They will hand over the terrorists, or they will share in their fate."[7]
>
> —President George W. Bush

Less than a week later, on September 20, President Bush addressed Congress and the American people. "On September the 11th," he said grimly, "enemies of freedom committed an act of war against our country." He identified the culprits as members of al Qaeda, which had its main training camps in Afghanistan, then ruled by an ultraconservative Muslim group called the Taliban. The Taliban must close those camps and hand over Bin Laden to the United States, Bush insisted. "These demands are not open to negotiation or discussion. The Taliban must act, and act immediately. They will hand over the terrorists, or they will share in their fate."[7]

In the same speech, Bush used the term *war on terror*, saying, "Our war on terror begins with al Qaeda, but it does not end there. It will not end until every terrorist group of global reach has been found, stopped and defeated."[8] In the days and weeks that followed, the Bush administration outlined a list of its goals for that audacious and challenging undertaking. The primary aim, of course, was to defeat the terrorists who had perpetuated the 9/11 attacks.

Another goal was to strengthen the international effort to fight terrorism. This included stopping the flow of weapons and supplies to terrorist groups; reducing the underlying conditions that terrorists seek to exploit, such as poverty and a lack of education; beefing up security in the United States; and protecting Americans and their allies overseas. "The war against global terror will be hard and long," Bush said in a later public announcement. "Today, terror cells exist on nearly every continent and in dozens of countries, including our own." Victory "will be measured through the steady, patient work of dismantling terror networks and bringing terrorists to justice, often-times one by one."[9]

The Invasions of Afghanistan and Iraq

US officials were not surprised when the Taliban refused to hand over Bin Laden and crack down on al Qaeda and its training camps. In response, on October 7, 2001, Americans conducted air strikes against key targets in Afghanistan. US soldiers were soon on the ground, and that nation's capital, Kabul, was under American control by mid-November. US allies, including Great Britain, also sent troops to Afghanistan in the weeks and months that followed.

In the face of these superior forces, Taliban leaders and their hard-core supporters, along with Bin Laden and his lieutenants, fled into the rugged mountains of eastern Afghanistan. Over the course of a few weeks, occasional skirmishes occurred between the allies and members of the Taliban and al Qaeda. At a place in the mountains called Tora Bora, Bin Laden narrowly escaped capture and managed to slip away into Pakistan. Many of the Taliban also escaped into Pakistan, where they set up bases from which to stage raids into their home country in hopes of regaining control of it.

Some critics of Bush's handling of the US invasion of Afghanistan claimed that American strategic errors had allowed Bin Laden to get away. Criticism against the Bush administration grew even more heated beginning in 2003. In March of that year, Bush launched a large-scale US invasion of Iraq. He and his advisers rationalized this move by pointing out that Iraq had been on a US list of state sponsors of terrorism since 1990.

Critics countered this assertion by saying that Iraq and its leader, Saddam Hussein, had played no part in 9/11. But Bush claimed that Saddam Hussein had weapons of mass destruction (WMDs, meaning biological, chemical, and nuclear weapons), which could be used in terrorist attacks on other nations. Therefore, Bush claimed, entering Iraq, deposing Saddam Hussein, and seizing his WMDs had to be part of the War on Terror.

US forces did remove Saddam Hussein from power. But a thorough search of Iraq by weapons inspectors from the United Nations

Bill Clinton Declares War on Terror?

George W. Bush was not the first US president to recognize that the United States was caught in an ongoing struggle against international terrorism. In August 1996, a little more than five years before 9/11 and the official start of the War on Terror, President Bill Clinton stated in a speech at a major American university,

> This will be a long, hard struggle. There will be setbacks along the way. But just as no enemy could drive us from the fight to meet our challenges and protect our values in World War II and the Cold War, we will not be driven from the tough fight against terrorism today. Terrorism is the enemy of our generation, and we must prevail. [But] I want to make it clear to the American people that while we can defeat terrorists, it will be a long time before we defeat terrorism. America will remain a target because we are uniquely present in the world, because we act to advance peace and democracy, because we have taken a tougher stand against terrorism, and because we are the most open society on earth. But to change any of that, to pull our troops back from the world's trouble spots, to turn our backs on those taking risks for peace, to weaken our opposition against terrorism, to curtail the freedom that is our birthright, would be to give terrorism the victory it must not and will not have.

William J. Clinton, "Remarks on International Security Issues at George Washington University, August 5, 1996," American Presidency Project. www.presidency.ucsb.edu.

and US soldiers found no WMDs. In addition the democratic government that US officials helped the Iraqis install proved weak and unable to quell an insurgency that soon erupted in various areas of the country. Insurgency members opposed the ongoing US occupation of Iraq as well as the new local government. The insurrection resulted in many thousands of Iraqi and American deaths in the years that followed.

US soldiers move through a portion of Baghdad, Iraq. The successful US-led invasion of that nation in 2003 brought down the dictatorship of Saddam Hussein, but it also brought out many critics who saw no connection between Iraq and the terrorists responsible for 9/11.

Terror Across the Globe

Meanwhile, terrorism continued outside of Iraq's borders. Sometimes al Qaeda or other groups affiliated with it were responsible. In other cases the culprits were new terrorist organizations inspired by al Qaeda or those that wanted to gain political power in specific nations. These violent incidents occurred more often in some countries than in others.

Pakistan suffered far more than most. Between 2001 and 2011, for example, thousands of Pakistanis were killed in hundreds of terrorist-related incidents. The reasons for this carnage varied. Some of the violence was perpetrated by al Qaeda–affiliated groups angry at Pakistan's government for helping the United States with its War on Terror. Other terrorist acts were the work of Muslim extremists who wanted to destabilize and take over Pakistan.

One of the most horrific international terrorist attacks during this period occurred on the Indonesian island of Bali in October 2002. A huge bomb blast leveled a local nightclub, killing 202 people. Among the victims were 88 Australians, 38 Indonesians, and individuals from twenty other countries. Another 209 people were injured by the blast. These killings were the work of Jemaah Islamiya, an Indonesian radical group inspired by al Qaeda and the Taliban.

Other notable terrorist bombings rocked nations around the world in the next dozen years. Among the more destructive were those that struck Casablanca, Morocco, and Istanbul, Turkey, in 2003; Madrid, Spain, in 2004; London, Great Britain, in 2005; Algiers, Algeria, and Glasgow, Scotland, in 2007; Marrakech, Morocco, in 2011; and various parts of France in 2012 and 2015.

Horror at Fort Hood

Several episodes of domestic terrorism—acts by American citizens inspired by foreign terrorist groups—happened within US borders. One of the bloodiest of these events took place on November 5, 2009, at the US Army base in Fort Hood, Texas. Major Nidal Malik Hasan, an army psychiatrist who had grown up in Virginia, had been a loyal American soldier. But over time he had become convinced that the international war against terrorism was actually a war against his religion, Islam. Believing this claim made by al Qaeda and a number of other terrorist organizations, Hasan armed himself with a semiautomatic pistol. Entering a Fort Hood processing center where soldiers who were about to be sent to duty posts overseas had assembled, he suddenly yelled out, "Allahu Akbar," Arabic for "God is great." Then he opened fire at the people milling about inside the center. Thirteen individuals were killed and more than thirty others were wounded. The incident was the worst case of mass murder ever at a US military installation. Wounded by a civilian police officer, Hasan was captured and later sentenced to death by a military court.

A Strategic Antiterrorist Vision

Though many terrorist mass killings occurred, terrorism experts say that many other plots intended to wreak havoc failed. For example, between 2001 and 2015, at least seventy-five major terrorist plots against the United States were thwarted. In part these plots were stopped because of increasingly effective Western antiterrorism efforts. According to a noted American think tank, "The U.S. has come a long way in terms of its readiness to prevent and combat acts of terrorism. Large investments in the Department of Homeland Security (DHS), the FBI, the intelligence community, state and local partners, and other government agencies have increased the U.S.'s ability to prevent terrorism before it strikes."[10]

Despite these successes, however, a few older terrorist groups, most notably al Qaeda, continue to pose threats to this day, and new terrorist organizations crop up on a regular basis. Their episodic assaults on various global targets add to the overall death toll associated with the ongoing fight against terrorism. Between 2001 and 2011 alone, some thirty-five thousand people died as a result of terrorist attacks and military actions launched to bring the perpetrators to justice. In that same period, economic losses as a result of terrorist attacks plus the cost of antiterrorism efforts worldwide totaled a staggering $68 billion.

Because terrorism continues to have a significant impact on nations around the world, strategies to fight it continue, although most international officials no longer call their antiterrorist efforts the War on Terror. According to leading Western experts on terrorism, Americans and their allies must be ready to counter any and all violent fanatical groups that threaten democracy and freedom. As the Rand Corporation, a US global policy think tank, puts it, "In light of the global increase in the number and lethality of terrorist attacks, it has become imperative that nations, states, and private citizens become more involved in a strategic vision to recognize, prepare for, and—if possible—prevent such events."[11]

CHAPTER TWO

How Did the 9/11 Attacks Launch the War on Terror?

Focus Questions

1. Why do you think the US government decided that military action was the best response to the 9/11 terrorist attacks?
2. What actions other than using military force might the United States have used in answer to the 9/11 terrorist attacks?
3. Do you think it is ethical for nations to use force against sponsors of terrorism even though those entities do not actually commit the attacks? Why or why not?

The War on Terror that President George W. Bush launched was a direct response to the terrorist attacks against New York City and Washington, DC, on September 11, 2001. A small band of al Qaeda operatives killed close to three thousand people in the course of a few hours and destroyed iconic American buildings.

The attacks were so brazen, so enormous in scope, and so destructive it seemed impossible that any sitting US government would allow them to go unpunished. And surely the horrified and furious American people would expect the government to act. The director of the Central Intelligence Agency (CIA) at the time, George J. Tenet, summed up the situation well. Speaking to a gathering of his officers and other workers on the day following the attacks, he said, "Yesterday, the entire American people—joined by men and women around the globe—recoiled in horror at the barbaric acts against our country." Visibly upset, he added, "The bloody hand of evil struck again and again, stealing thousands of innocent lives. As the devastating toll of terror comes into focus, we are sure to find among those who were lost friends, colleagues, and others we hold dear."[12]

Although the victims must be mourned, Tenet went on, Americans must also consider how to respond to the outrage the terrorists had perpetrated. Amid the "numbing shock" and "profound grief," he stated, there was also "renewed resolve" to strike back. "As President Bush said last night," Tenet asserted, "the search for the sponsors of these unspeakable acts has already begun. Our Agency is among the leaders of that search."[13] The hunt for the attacks' sponsors, as Tenet called them, proved to be the opening salvo in the ensuing War on Terror.

"We're Flying Way Too Low"

Tenet's use of words such as *horror*, *barbaric*, and *numbing shock* to describe the 9/11 attacks perfectly captured the reactions of individuals of all walks of life around the world. A brief overview of the 9/11 events makes clear why most people reacted in horror and why they demanded a forceful military response.

In New York City's Manhattan borough, Tuesday, September 11, 2001, began as most weekdays did. The streets stretching between the numerous skyscrapers were alive with taxis and buses, and the sidewalks teemed with men and women about to begin their workday. Because of the usual underlying drone of city noise, the sound of an airplane flying too low overhead escaped most people's attention.

That plane—an American Airlines Boeing 767—flew southward along the Hudson River. At that moment, one of the nine flight attendants aboard, Madeline Sweeney, was on the phone with a Boston-based American Airlines official, Michael Woodward. Not long before, she had anxiously informed him that the plane had been hijacked. Now she told him that the aircraft had changed direction and was heading over the city's skyline. Sweeney reported, "I see the buildings" and "we're flying way too low," after which she paused. Then, quietly, and with sudden realization in her voice, she said, "Oh, my God!"[14]

What Woodward did not yet know was that directly after Swee-ney had spoken those three words, at exactly 8:45 a.m., the aircraft plunged into the eightieth floor of the World Trade Center's north tower. The plane's thousands of gallons of jet fuel ignited, creating a monstrous fireball that incinerated all aboard, along with hundreds of people in the building's surrounding offices. The fire then spread swiftly, trapping hundreds more in the building's upper floors.

Soon television networks and other media outlets began broad-casting live shots of the damaged structure. Reporters initially told the public that a plane, apparently flying off course, had accidentally struck the building. But that explanation was shown to be incorrect only minutes later. At 9:13 a.m., in full view of thousands of cameras, a second commercial airliner struck the World Trade Center's south tower near the sixtieth floor.

The crash of aircraft hitting the World Trade Center produced fiery explosions and a cascade of wreckage. Nearby onlookers' initial shock gave way to panic when the Twin Towers soon fell and huge clouds of dust and debris billowed through the surrounding streets.

The Origins of the Term
War on Terror

The exact derivation of the term *war on terror* to describe the conflict against al Qaeda ignited by 9/11 is still somewhat uncertain. Many historians assume that President George W. Bush coined the term in his speech delivered to Congress and the nation on September 20, 2001. In that speech, he stated, "Our war on terror begins with al Qaeda, but it does not end there." However, other experts disagree and suggest that Bush's speechwriter was inspired by one or more other sources. For example, some point to a statement made in 1984 by White House officials in President Ronald Reagan's administration. Hoping to help pass legislation intended to freeze the assets of terrorist groups, they said there was a war against terrorism going on. Another theory holds that the term *war on terror* was based on noted newsman Tom Brokaw's on-air remarks right after the World Trade Center's south tower collapsed on September 11, 2001. Brokaw exclaimed, "Terrorists have declared war on [America]." Still another view suggests that President Bush did coin the phrase but did so informally on September 16 rather than in his televised September 20 address. On September 16, in an off-the-cuff comment to reporters, Bush said, "This crusade—this war on terrorism—is going to take a while." Whatever the origins of the term *war on terror* might be, in 2007 the British government officially abandoned it, and in 2013 President Barack Obama did the same.

George W. Bush, "Address to Congress and the American People Following the Sept. 11, 2001 Attacks." www.history2u.com.

Tom Brokaw, "Breaking News on September 11th," NBC Learn. https://archives.nbclearn.com.

Qoted in Kenneth R. Bazinet, "A Fight vs. Evil, Bush and Cabinet Tell U.S.," *New York Daily News*, September 17, 2001. www.nydailynews.com/archives.

A Series of Horrifying Events

It was clear now that New York City, and perhaps the United States itself, was under deliberate attack. Aviation and military experts noted that two planes crashing into the World Trade Center only minutes apart could not be an accident or a coincidence.

Still more proof that the country had been deliberately attacked came at 9:45 a.m., when a third passenger plane smashed into the US military's central administrative hub, the Pentagon, in Washington, DC. More than 120 people were killed. A fourth hijacked airliner crashed in a Pennsylvania field, killing all on board. Investigators later learned that the terrorists in control of it had intended to fly the plane into the US Capitol or the White House. But the passengers had managed to disrupt the terrorists, who either lost control of or purposely crashed the plane.

The day's series of horrifying events continued. Fifteen minutes after the third plane struck the Pentagon, in chaos-filled Manhattan the World Trade Center's still-burning south tower abruptly collapsed. Massive clouds of crushed concrete, glass, wood, and human remains billowed outward, coating everything with that awful mix. Making matters worse, half an hour later the north tower also collapsed, producing another toxic cloud of debris.

The death toll from the catastrophic events of that morning was not known for sure at first. But federal, state, and local authorities eventually confirmed that almost three thousand people had lost their lives during the attacks and their immediate aftermath. Among the dead were 343 firefighters and paramedics and 60 New York City police and Port Authority officers. These courageous individuals had rushed to the stricken towers in an effort to help and had become victims themselves. In addition to the death toll, nearly 10,000 people were injured.

"The Steel of American Resolve"

In the wake of the 9/11 events, the biggest question on the minds of all Americans was who could have committed this horrifying crime? It did not take long for US intelligence personnel to discover that the offenders were nineteen Muslim men who were either members of al Qaeda or had done that terrorist group's bidding. This scenario was later confirmed when that organization's leader, Osama bin Laden, took credit for the disaster. He said the attacks were meant as retribution for US support for Israel and America's ongoing military presence in Middle Eastern Arabic countries.

Immediate reactions across the United States were predictably loud and angry. Americans of all ages, professions, and political leanings looked to the federal government for statements about retaliation. "The mood of the nation after 9/11," Pepperdine University scholar Wesley B. Truitt points out, "was uniformly clear: strike back at al Qaeda with the full force and fury of the United States."[15]

President Bush did not disappoint. On the evening of September 11 he spoke to the nation, saying,

> Today, our fellow citizens, our way of life, our very freedom came under attack in a series of deliberate and deadly terrorist acts. The victims were in airplanes, or in their offices; secretaries, businessmen and women, military and federal workers; moms and dads, friends and neighbors. Thousands of lives were suddenly ended by evil, despicable acts of terror.[16]

The president went on to say that the many photos of airliners crashing into buildings, collapsing structures, and other carnage had quite naturally made Americans sad and angry. The despicable attacks had been meant to "frighten our nation into chaos and retreat," he stated. But the terrorists had failed in that regard. Americans were too strong and righteous to submit, Bush argued. Instead, he said, "a great people has been moved to defend a great nation. Terrorist attacks can shake the foundations of our biggest buildings, but they cannot touch the foundation of America. These acts shattered steel, but they cannot dent the steel of American resolve."[17]

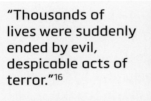

"Thousands of lives were suddenly ended by evil, despicable acts of terror."[16]

—President George W. Bush

The Authorization to Use Force

The next day President Bush met with his national security team. He told the experts assembled that the assaults on New York City and Washington, DC, were more than mere terrorist acts. They were also "acts of war." Indeed, he stated, "freedom and democracy are under attack." Moreover, he asserted that "this enemy attacked not just *our*

An Afghan soldier uses a stick to maintain order among a group of women waiting in line. The treatment of women under the Taliban was one of the reasons President Bush provided to justify America's opposition to the regime that he blamed for supporting al Qaeda.

people, but all freedom-loving people everywhere in the world. The United States of America will use all our resources to conquer this enemy. We will rally the world. We will be patient, we will be focused, and we will be steadfast in our determination."[18]

Bush's references to "acts of war" and "conquering" the enemy were clear indications that he envisioned using military force against the terrorists. He was aware that he had the backing of the vast majority of Americans, who shared his defiant attitude. The president was pleased to find that that outlook was reflected as well in nearly all members of the US Congress, whose authorization to use force he now sought. The US Constitution states that the power to declare war lies with Congress rather than the chief executive. The president can send soldiers into battle without congressional approval. But for political reasons, presidents almost always try to legitimize their use of force by getting such approval, even if not in the form of a formal war declaration.

On September 14, 2001, a mere three days after 9/11, representatives and senators met to consider granting the president's request. With no significant debate in either the Senate or the House of Representatives, in a matter of hours the two chambers of Congress hammered out a joint resolution granting the president authorization to use military force (AUMF) in the upcoming battle against the terrorists. In its preamble, the resolution stated that "acts of treacherous violence were committed against the United States and its citizens." Therefore, it was both necessary and fitting that the nation "exercise its rights to self-defense and to protect United States citizens both at home and abroad."[19]

The wording of the section granting legal congressional approval of the use of force was straightforward. "The President," it began, "is authorized to use all necessary and appropriate force against those nations, organizations, or persons he determines planned, authorized, committed, or aided the terrorist attacks that occurred on September 11, 2001."[20] Furthermore, anyone who had harbored the terrorists, or might harbor them in the future, would also be considered guilty of attacking the United States.

The resolution passed in the Senate by a roll call vote. A roll call vote is a procedure in which a clerk calls out the senators' names one by one, and each answers either "aye" or "nay." Out of the possible one hundred votes, one for each senator, the total was ninety-eight ayes and zero nays. (For undisclosed reasons of their own, two senators did not vote.) Such unanimity in that lawmaking body is rare, which prompted Senator Trent Lott of Mississippi to remark, "The Senate [was] united like I have never seen it before."[21] In the House, meanwhile, the total was 420 ayes, 1 nay, and 10 who did not vote. The nay vote was cast by Barbara Lee of California, who felt that the resolution's wording was too broad and gave the president a bit too much power.

> "The Senate [was] united like I have never seen it before."[21]
>
> —Mississippi senator Trent Lott

Barbara Lee Explains Her "Nay" Vote

When the US House of Representatives passed its resolution on September 14, 2001, to authorize President Bush to use force against the terrorists responsible for the 9/11 attacks, only one congressperson voted no. That individual was Barbara Lee of California's thirteenth congressional district.

Born July 16, 1946, she was the first woman to represent the thirteenth district. Lee's decision to vote no on the authorization to use military force was based on her opinion that the powers it granted the president were too broad. She later explained, saying,

> It was a blank check to the president to attack anyone involved in the September 11 events—anywhere, in any country, without regard to our nation's long-term foreign policy, economic and national security interests, and without time limit. In granting these overly broad powers, the Congress failed its responsibility to understand the dimensions of its declaration. I could not support such a grant of war-making authority to the president. I believe it would put more innocent lives at risk. The president has the constitutional authority to protect the nation from further attack, and he has mobilized the armed forces to do just that. The Congress should have waited for the facts to be presented and then acted with fuller knowledge of the consequences of our action.

Barbara Lee, "Why I Opposed the Resolution to Authorize Force," *San Francisco Chronicle*, September 23, 2001. www.sfgate.com.

George Bush Versus the Taliban

President Bush signed the AUMF four days later, on September 18. Two days after that he delivered his now-famous address to Congress, the American people, and the world. In the speech, he revealed at least some of the general strategy that he and his military generals would use in the War on Terror in the months and years ahead.

The first thing the president did was identify the initial US targets in that conflict. True, he said, Bin Laden and his al Qaeda followers seemed to have perpetrated the recent attacks. But that terrorist group was presently under the protection of the Taliban, Afghanistan's ultra-conservative ruling party. "Al Qaeda has great influence in Afghanistan," he explained, "and supports the Taliban regime." In that country, he went on,

> we see al Qaeda's vision for the world. Afghanistan's people have been brutalized. Many are starving and many have fled. Women are not allowed to attend school. You can be jailed for owning a television. Religion can be practiced only as their leaders dictate. [We] condemn the Taliban regime. It is not only repressing its own people, it is threatening people everywhere by sponsoring and sheltering and supplying terrorists.[22]

Bush then called on the Taliban to cooperate with the United States. He asserted that the government must hand over al Qaeda's leaders, protect foreign journalists and diplomats in their nation, and permanently close every terrorist training camp in Afghanistan. The Taliban's immediate response to these demands was to make a demand of its own. Its leaders told Bush that he must provide them with specific evidence of Bin Laden's involvement in the 9/11 attacks. If any such proof existed, they claimed they would themselves try Bin Laden in an Islamic court, but they would never hand him over to American authorities.

In the days that followed, President Bush categorically refused to comply with the Taliban's demand. Instead, he formed a coalition of willing allies, chief among them the United Kingdom. On October 7, 2001, he ordered coalition forces to enter Afghanistan, remove the Taliban from power, and track down Bin Laden. The War on Terror that Bush had first described in his September 20 speech as a necessary response to the 9/11 attacks had now officially begun.

An Enemy That Hides

The initial salvo in the invasion of Afghanistan consisted of a series of coalition bombing raids that struck the capital, Kabul, and key Tali-

American bomber planes prepare to launch from the aircraft carrier USS *Carl Vinson* on October 7, 2001. Their mission was to soften up Taliban targets and pave the way for US, British, and anti-Taliban Afghan ground forces to quickly overpower enemy resistance.

ban military installations. As the days wore on, the damage became extensive. It was clear that the Taliban forces were weakened and running scared. On October 15, eight days after the invasion had begun, a Taliban spokesman sent a message to US leaders. If the Americans stopped the bombing, he said, "we would be ready to hand him [Bin Laden] over to a third country." He added, "If America were to step back from the current policy, then we could negotiate. Then we could discuss which third country."[23]

President Bush flatly turned this offer down, emphasizing that the bombing would stop only if his own initial demands were met. In the weeks that followed, fighting in Afghanistan's mountainous southern region intensified. US forces came close to capturing Bin Laden, but he and his lieutenants stealthily escaped into Pakistan. Bin Laden's actions seemed to confirm what President Bush had told his security team shortly after 9/11: "The American people need to know that we're facing a different enemy than we have ever faced.

This enemy hides in shadows, and has no regard for human life. This is an enemy who preys on innocent and unsuspecting people, then runs for cover."[24]

Although Bin Laden had managed to elude the coalition forces hunting for him, those forces were determined to keep up the search. President Bush set the tone for the ensuing War on Terror when he pointed out that al Qaeda "won't be able to run for cover forever." He added, "This is an enemy that thinks its harbors are safe. But they won't be safe forever." The battle against al Qaeda would require time and determination, he said. "But make no mistake about it: we will win."[25] That victory did not come during Bush's term in office, however, and the fight between the United States and al Qaeda continues.

CHAPTER THREE

How Did the Killing of Osama bin Laden Weaken al Qaeda?

Focus Questions

1. Why do you think individuals such as Osama bin Laden can influence others to do their bidding, even to kill?
2. What might have happened had the United States not given Bin Laden a proper Islamic burial?
3. In your view, why is vindication, such as the killing of Bin Laden, so important to the families of victims?

In the initial few years following the 9/11 attacks, al Qaeda, headed by Bin Laden, appeared to be a major threat to Western countries, including the United States. However, as American terrorism expert Richard A. Clarke pointed out, that terrorist organization itself was only part of the problem. New terrorist groups—in a sense clones of al Qaeda—swiftly began imitating its anti-Western and anti-American position. Bin Laden's group, Clarke stated in 2004,

> was like a Hydra [a mythological monster with multiple heads], growing new heads. There have been far more major terrorist attacks by al Qaeda and its regional clones in the thirty months since September 11 than there were in the thirty months prior to that momentous event. I wonder if bin Laden and his deputies actually planned for September 11 to be like smashing a pod of seeds that spread around the world, allowing them to step back out of the picture and have the regional organizations they created take their generation-long struggle to the next level.[26]

Each of the new terrorist groups Clarke mentioned had a leader. But in the public's mind, as well as in the minds of US antiterrorism officials, one of those leaders stood above all the others. The symbolic, if not actual, chief of all those terrorist groups was Bin Laden. It therefore became an essential goal for US and other Western officials to eliminate Bin Laden. Hopefully, the reasoning went, if the Hydra's main head could be severed, no new ones would appear.

> "I wonder if bin Laden and his deputies actually planned for September 11 to be like smashing a pod of seeds that spread around the world."[26]
>
> —American counter-terrorism expert Richard A. Clarke

Even if Bin Laden could be eliminated, however, one burning question remained. Namely, how would al Qaeda itself be affected by his eradication? Would that organization be weakened and fall apart, or would it survive under new leadership?

The Escape from Tora Bora

Efforts to capture or kill Bin Laden began shortly after 9/11. Indeed, one of the chief aims of American military action in Afghanistan beginning in October 2001 was to find and eliminate Bin Laden. To that end, US intelligence operatives tracked Bin Laden to the region of Tora Bora in Afghanistan's remote southern mountains.

Having finally identified the terrorist's position, an American-led four-man team of CIA agents and US special forces, aided by ten Afghans, entered the area. They discovered that Bin Laden had taken refuge in a large complex of caves, accompanied by as many as nine hundred al Qaeda fighters. The American team's leader, Gary Berntsen, contacted his superiors by phone. He requested that hundreds of US soldiers be sent in immediately to make sure Bin Laden did not escape into nearby Pakistan.

For reasons that are still unclear, however, those reinforcements never arrived, and Bin Laden did slip away into Pakistan. An angry Berntsen later said, "The U.S. military spends a trillion dollars a year on defense. Why is it that they could not get forces into that area?"[27] Speaking for many military experts, Clarke agrees that the operation

Anti-Taliban Afghan soldiers sit outside the al Qaeda stronghold of Tora Bora in the White Mountains of eastern Afghanistan. CIA operatives and Special Forces aided friendly Afghans in clearing out the massive cave complex where Bin Laden had sought shelter.

was bungled. "Tora Bora was just a case of military incompetence,"[28] he argues.

After the Tora Bora episode, Bin Laden dropped out of sight so completely that US and other Western intelligence agencies could not pinpoint his whereabouts. This happened in part because he had plenty of help. American terrorism experts point out that there existed (and still exists) within Pakistan a network of people who hated Americans as much as Bin Laden did. They quietly moved him from one safe house to another so that he could elude the United States and its allies.

A Proper Islamic Funeral

Eventually, however, new clues to Bin Laden's location surfaced. Late in 2010 US intelligence received tips from anonymous sources in the Middle East. Not only was the al Qaeda chieftain still in Pakistan, the sources suggested, he was living in a house in the small city of

Abbottabad. Secret US satellite photos revealed that the house rested within a large compound surrounded by tall concrete walls topped by barbed wire. The compound measured some 8,000 square feet (743 sq. m), about one-sixth the size of a football field, and had two sturdy security gates.

In February 2011, US intelligence became convinced that Bin Laden was hiding in the compound, and President Barack Obama decided to act. He ordered one of the top US special forces groups—the Navy SEALs—to start intense secret training for a crucial upcoming mission. Soon they learned that they would be entering Pakistan under the cover of night and killing Bin Laden.

The SEALs' training left nothing to chance. They employed a full-size replica of the Pakistani compound in which to practice infiltrating the compound and seizing Bin Laden. When they felt they were ready to go, President Obama sent them to the Middle East and gave the go-ahead for the mission, code-named Operation Neptune Spear.

> "I'm happy that justice was done. I'm happy that we as a country have been vindicated."[29]
>
> —A 9/11 widow reacting to Osama bin Laden's death

On May 2, 2011, the commandos flew quietly through the darkened Pakistani skies in a small squadron of Black Hawk stealth helicopters. Reaching the target, they executed the mission with few hitches. After killing some guards, they located Bin Laden and shot him dead, then carried his body to the aircraft carrier USS *Carl Vinson* in the northern Arabian Sea. There, the leading perpetrator of the 9/11 terrorist attacks was buried at sea, after those involved carefully ensured that he had a proper Islamic funeral.

A Father Figure Removed

When President Obama announced that Bin Laden had been killed during a US raid, most Americans were relieved and even happy. Particularly moved were the relatives of people who had been killed during the 9/11 attacks. "I know we're not supposed to be joyful at someone's death," remarked the widow of a man who died in the collapse of the World Trade Center towers. But she went on to say, "I'm happy that justice was done. I'm happy that we as a country have been

Bin Laden's Burial at Sea

After killing al Qaeda founder Osama bin Laden in Pakistan, the Navy SEALs transported his body to the USS *Carl Vinson,* which was waiting in the northern Arabian Sea. President Obama and his advisers had decided in advance of the raid that it would be best to give Bin Laden a sea burial. That would be better than a land burial, they reasoned, because a land grave might become a shrine frequently visited by Bin Laden's followers. In disposing of the body, US Navy personnel made sure to follow proper Islamic funeral rites. A White House official later explained that "the burial of bin Laden's remains was done in strict conformance with Islamic precepts and practices," after consulting with Islamic experts. Those handling the body washed it according to accepted Islamic custom, wrapped it in a white sheet, and placed both inside a weighted bag, the official said. A tiny group of witnesses then watched as a military officer read prepared religious remarks in a dignified manner, which an Arabic native speaker translated. Finally, some of those involved eased the body bag into the sea. The White House official told reporters that the Obama administration followed this procedure partly because Americans always treat the bodies of enemy dead with human decency. Also, it seemed important not to give surviving al Qaeda terrorists a propaganda tool. They would not be able to claim ever afterward that the United States had disrespected and mistreated Bin Laden's remains out of hatred for him.

Quoted in John Ireland and Elisabeth Bumiller, "Islamic Scholars Split over Sea Burial for Bin Laden," *New York Times*, May 2, 2011. www.nytimes.com.

---

vindicated, that we will not tolerate what was done to us. Every day of my life is 9/11. I close the door to my house, and my husband is not there [because] of this man [Bin Laden]. If God wants to forgive him, that's God. I can't."[29]

In addition to such emotional reactions to Bin Laden's death, many people logically concluded that Bin Laden's elimination would have positive practical consequences. Authorities on antiterrorism agreed that al Qaeda had been weakened in various ways. First, that

On May 2, 2011, President Obama announced to the world that Osama bin Laden had been killed during a raid on a compound in Abbottabad, Pakistan. Many felt relief that America's number one enemy had been found, but Bin Laden's death did not end the fight against al Qaeda.

group had lost its primary inspiration for new recruits. According to this view, as long as Bin Laden was alive and instigating terrorist operations, Muslims who distrusted Western nations had a sort of father figure to revere.

But thanks to the raid by the Navy SEALs, that inspiration was gone. "Bin Laden was a very special figure," University of Maryland terrorism expert Arie Kruglanski explains. "He proved himself in battle, he sacrificed his material interests for the cause, and he was able to organize spectacular attacks against the United States and its allies." Seen from the perspective of his sympathizers, those traits would be very difficult to find in others, making Bin Laden a unique and irreplaceable leader. So his passing was "likely to considerably harm al Qaeda's ability to turn enthusiastic youths to the cause of jihad [Islamic holy war]."[30]

The CIA's former national intelligence officer for southern Asia, Paul Pillar, agrees. "Precisely because he [Bin Laden] had such symbolic status in the eyes of his followers," Pillar says, "it was important that he was brought to justice."[31] This view has also been echoed by Philip Mudd, a former antiterrorism expert for the Federal Bureau of Investigation. "In the context of a lot of other strikes targeting top al-Qaida leadership," he points out, "bin Laden's death may have been the blow that started the foundation of that organization really crumbling."[32]

A number of experts also point out that President Obama's steadfast and eventually successful efforts to track down Bin Laden discredited one of al Qaeda's chief propaganda tools. For years Bin Laden and other terrorist leaders had argued that the United States and its allies lacked the will to wage a long struggle against al Qaeda and against terrorism in general. But the death of al Qaeda's supreme leader, Kruglanski says, changed that. It thoroughly disproved the notion that the West "has a short attention span and lacks the patience and persistence to win the struggle."[33]

> "Precisely because he [Bin Laden] had such symbolic status in the eyes of his followers, it was important that he was brought to justice."[31]
>
> —Paul Pillar, a former CIA officer for southern Asia

A Treasure Trove of Data

Still more evidence of how Bin Laden's death negatively affected al Qaeda came from some of the materials the SEALs seized during their raid of the compound in Abbottabad. After killing Bin Laden, some of the commandos carried his body to their waiting helicopter. Meanwhile, most of the other SEALs scoured the buildings in the compound, searching for information about al Qaeda that Bin Laden may have had in his possession. They took computers, thumb drives, written records, videos, and more.

These materials revealed that Bin Laden had been hoarding a treasure trove of information about al Qaeda's inner workings, its operatives, its plans, and its financial dealings. Regarding the latter, the captured records showed that that organization had been experiencing money troubles for some time. It became clear that for a while after 9/11, which was a big propaganda coup for al Qaeda, it had received funds from various secret sources in the Arab world. But over time

American, British, and other allied counterterrorism forces had forced Bin Laden and his lieutenants to go on the run. During those same years several al Qaeda leaders had been killed. These events had caused some of those initial financial sources to dry up, and US officials were certain that Bin Laden's death would choke off even more money.

Other important data seized during the raid concerned al Qaeda's organization and the aims of its various chapters and affiliates around the globe. Before and just after 9/11, the records revealed, Bin Laden's group had been fairly small, centralized, and tightly organized. But in the months and years that followed, it splintered into diverse branches and factions. At first some of those groups took orders, or at least advice, from the original, central al Qaeda hub. But over time leaders of the outlying groups tended to make their own decisions and plans.

Due to a loosening of the original group's control, Bin Laden's power had steadily declined. He was still respected as a sort of figurehead and father figure, but he no longer called all the shots. One result of his loss of control was his inability to stop some of the outlying al Qaeda leaders from getting involved in squabbles with other Muslim groups in their local areas. According to Kruglanski, several of those assorted al Qaeda affiliates seemed "to be less interested in attacking the West than in local struggles."[34]

Similarly, in the immediate wake of Bin Laden's death, al Qaeda as a whole became less focused and less effective as an opponent of Western nations. Its "enterprise is more decentralized," political commentator Brian Michael Jenkins states. "Its organizational survival now heavily depends on its Taliban allies in Afghanistan, on its affiliates, and on its ability to inspire homegrown terrorists." Moreover, "some studies show that decapitation [removing its main leader] decreases the number of [the group's] attacks and [its] success rates."[35]

Crippling Losses

Those scattered al Qaeda affiliates were affected by Bin Laden's death in another way as well. Even before the SEALs assassinated him, several of Bin Laden's lieutenants, including the heads of some of the subordinate chapters, had been killed by US soldiers and other Western operatives. After his elimination, that trend intensified. "There's little doubt that the Abbottabad raid landed a potentially crippling blow" against al Qaeda, noted journalist James Kitfield writes. The SEALs' raid

> was followed by a series of successful strikes against senior bin Laden lieutenants. In fact, in roughly the [year following the raid] U.S. intelligence officials claim to have killed half of al-Qaida's top 20 leaders in raids and attacks by armed drones, including Ilyas Kashmiri, considered one of al-Qaida's most dangerous operational commanders and strategists, [and] Anwar al-Awlaki, the American-born leader of al-Qaida in the Arabian Peninsula and a Jihadist propagandist that many counterterrorism experts considered nearly as dangerous as bin Laden himself.[36]

After the death of Bin Laden, leadership of al Qaeda fell to Ayman al-Zawahiri (at left), an Egyptian who had served as Bin Laden's adviser. Al-Zawahiri has since remained hidden, and the United States continues to offer a $25 million reward for information concerning his location.

After the deaths of these and other al Qaeda bosses, by early 2017 the group's primary surviving leader was Ayman al-Zawahiri, Bin Laden's former deputy and number-two man. Numerous US antiterrorist experts have pointed out that al-Zawahiri remains a formidable foe. He continues to despise Western nations, they warn, especially the United States. However, the overall consensus is that al-Zawahiri may be less dangerous than Bin Laden was. "Al-Zawahiri has attempted to rebuild al-Qaida's core and reconstitute links to its global franchises, with uncertain results," Kitfield says. "By most accounts the taciturn [quiet and aloof] Zawahiri lacks bin Laden's personal appeal and charisma [charm and appeal] in uniting disparate extremist groups and rallying new recruits to al-Qaida's banner."[37]

The Killing of Anwar al-Awlaki

Among the many al Qaeda leaders killed by the United States and its allies in the wake of Osama bin Laden's death was Anwar al-Awlaki. Born in 1971 in New Mexico to Yemeni parents, he grew up in the United States. Later in life he became radicalized and began supporting al Qaeda's war with the West. After going into hiding in Yemen in March 2009, al-Awlaki became a key figure in the group's Yemeni branch. According to US officials, he acted as a senior recruiter and motivator who also planned or helped to plan a number of al Qaeda terrorist operations. Eventually antiterrorist experts in the US government debated whether to kill al-Awlaki. It was a thorny issue because he was a US citizen. White House lawyers argued that as a military enemy of the country he was not protected by Executive Order 11905, which prohibits killing citizens for political reasons. Based on that reasoning, on April 6, 2010, President Obama authorized al-Awlaki's assassination. In the morning of September 30, 2011, al-Awlaki and a few of his al Qaeda associates stopped to eat breakfast beside a dirt road in Yemen's west-central mountains. The men did not realize that a US drone was recording their every move from high above. At the last minute one of them glimpsed something moving in the sky. Alarmed, they rose to run, but it was too late. A Hellfire missile fired from the drone annihilated them all on the spot.

The elimination of almost an entire generation of al Qaeda leaders crippled the group's global efforts against the West. Among those losses, the most notable of all was Bin Laden himself. "Today's al Qaeda is clearly a diminished threat and the killing of bin Laden certainly contributed to that,"[38] Jenkins states.

The Robin Hood of Terrorists

Former CIA analyst Bruce Reidel concurs. "There is no question," he says, that within a year after Bin Laden's demise al Qaeda's central core had been "devastated by his loss." This was largely "because he had achieved mythic status as the Robin Hood of international terrorism who the sheriff couldn't catch. And at the time of his death he was still the boss who ran the organization and kept its archives." Thanks to the efforts of President Obama and his antiterrorist task force, Reidel goes on, "that myth has been destroyed." He adds with an air of finality, "Bin Laden has been brought to justice!"[39]

Nevertheless, having made the case that Bin Laden's death weakened al Qaeda, Reidel, Pillar, Mudd, and other experts caution that the group is hardly harmless and no longer a menace. "Al Qaeda is still a global enterprise pursuing violent jihad and remains dedicated to attacking its 'far enemy,' the United States," Jenkins warns. "Decapitation clearly did not terminate al Qaeda's armed jihad."[40]

Jenkins points out what he and many other experts see as perhaps al Qaeda's biggest threat to Western countries. True, he says, following the deaths of Bin Laden and other leaders of the group, attacks on Western nations by al Qaeda's foreign-based chapters have been far fewer than before. However, the danger of Western-born, or homegrown, terrorists who are inspired by al Qaeda is now higher than in the past.

Indeed, antiterrorism authorities state, homegrown terrorists seem unbothered by the dispersion and weakening of al Qaeda's overseas affiliates. Some of these American-, British-, and French-born individuals have carried out their attacks on behalf of al Qaeda. One well-known example was the assault on the Paris offices of the French weekly magazine *Charlie Hebdo* in January 2015. "Was al Qaeda hurt by the demise of its charismatic leader?" Jenkins asks. "Certainly," he answers. "Is the world a safer place because of it? Probably not."[41]

CHAPTER FOUR

How Did the War on Terror Contribute to the Founding of ISIS?

Focus Questions

1. In your view, can a mission to control others through the use of violent means ever succeed in the long run? Why or why not?
2. What information about Iraq might have helped US leaders make better decisions in 2003?
3. Why do you think efforts to create democracies in Iraq and Syria failed?

ISIS is a group that has replaced al Qaeda as the best-known and perhaps most dangerous terrorist organization in the world. The group goes by several names. Its acronym stands for the Islamic State of Iraq and Syria. Some Western experts call it ISIL (the Islamic State of Iraq and the Levant); others prefer the shorter version IS (the Islamic State); and many residents of Arabic countries refer to the organization as DAESH, which is an acronym for the Arabic translation of the Islamic State of Iraq and the Levant.

The Goals, Methods, and Roots of ISIS

Whatever one chooses to call it, ISIS is best described as a fundamentalist (ultraconservative) group made up mostly of Sunni Muslims. (Sunnis compose one of the two leading sects of Islam, the other being Shia Muslims, or Shiites. The two divisions disagree on some aspects of basic Islamic doctrine and frequently come to blows over their differences.) ISIS, with its main centers of power in Syria and Iraq, regularly employs extreme methods to advance its goals.

Chief among those aims are to expel all Westerners from the Middle East and ultimately to convert all of humanity to its views and ranks. Among the extreme methods that members of ISIS use to further these goals are violence, including bombings, beheadings, and other terrorist acts; intimidation; ethnic cleansing (ridding selected areas of ethnic and religious populations); political propaganda; and blatant civil rights abuses.

ISIS originated within areas of Iraq that were predominantly Sunni before the United States invaded that nation in 2003. One of the many developments of that invasion was the fragmentation of Iraq's population into politically opposing groups. ISIS grew from one of those groups. Therefore, historians and antiterrorism experts say, its formation was a by-product of the 2003 invasion of Iraq, which itself

ISIS fighters parade through northern Syria where they have strong support among conservative Muslims opposed to the government of Bashar al-Assad. Besides taking part in the Syrian civil war, ISIS has claimed responsibility for numerous terrorist activities throughout the world.

was an offshoot of the War on Terror. As Birmingham City University scholar John Badahur Lamb puts it, 9/11

> changed history by leading to two American-led invasions as part of the Global War on Terrorism: Afghanistan and then Iraq. Whilst the Afghan campaign was initially successful and had the backing of the international community, the Iraq campaign would lead to a long-running insurgency and widespread sectarian violence between the two dominant strands of Islam present in the country.[42]

The members of one of those sects, Lamb continues, subsequently evolved into ISIS.

The Invasion of Iraq

When US forces entered Iraq in 2003, few people foresaw that a later development of that action would be the formation of a terrorist group even more lethal than al Qaeda. But as historians often point out, all of the wars humans have waged over the centuries have had at least some unintended consequences. To properly appreciate how ISIS was born, therefore, it is essential to begin with the 2003 US invasion of Iraq.

> "The terrorists have made it clear that Iraq is the central front in their war against humanity."[43]
>
> —President George W. Bush in December 2005

That military action was intended to be an integral part of the War on Terror. This fact was best expressed by the man who initiated both of those actions. In a speech delivered in Philadelphia in December 2005, President George W. Bush stated,

> The war on terror will take many turns, and the enemy must be defeated on every battlefield, from the streets of Western cities, to the mountains of Afghanistan, to the tribal regions of Pakistan, to the islands of Southeast Asia and to the Horn of Africa. Yet the terrorists have made it clear that Iraq is the central front in their war against humanity. So we must recognize Iraq as the central front in the war on terror.[43]

Bush Links Iraq to the War on Terror

Though historians say that ISIS's rise to power was a direct consequence of the US invasion and occupation of Iraq in 2003, President George W. Bush argued at the time that the invasion was necessary. In a December 2005 speech, he stated,

> By fighting the terrorists in Iraq, we are confronting a direct threat to the American people. And we will accept nothing less than complete victory. We are pursuing a comprehensive strategy in Iraq. Our goal is victory. And victory will be achieved when the terrorists and Saddamists can no longer threaten Iraq's democracy, when the Iraqi security forces can provide for the safety of their own citizens, and when Iraq is not a safe haven for terrorists to plot new attacks against our nation. Our strategy in Iraq has three elements. On the economic side, we're helping the Iraqis restore their infrastructure, reform their economy and build the prosperity that will give all Iraqis a stake in a free and peaceful Iraq. On the security side, coalition and Iraqi forces are on the offense against the enemy. We're working together to clear out areas controlled by the terrorists and Saddam loyalists, and leaving Iraqi forces to hold territory taken from the enemy. And as we help Iraqis fight these enemies, we're working to build capable and effective Iraqi security forces.

Quoted in *Washington Post*, "President Bush Delivers Remarks on the War on Terrorism, December 12, 2005." www.washingtonpost.com.

At the time that Bush ordered the incursion into Iraq in 2003, American society was sharply divided about whether it was a good idea. On one side were those who thought the invasion was necessary, as the president claimed, to fight terrorism. Others argued that terrorists were mostly in Afghanistan and elsewhere and that invading Iraq would be an unnecessary diversion from the War on Terror. Saddam Hussein was a brutal dictator, they admitted. But he was not a terrorist who might use nuclear weapons against the West, and, moreover, al Qaeda terrorist leader Osama bin Laden and Saddam Hussein actually despised each other.

As it turned out, those who were against Bush's invasion of Iraq were on the right side of history. The present consensus of the vast majority of historians and military experts is that the Iraq war was a mistake that actually ended up creating far more terrorists than it eliminated. National security researcher Loren Thompson sums up that view, saying that Iraq

> is a country of warring ethnic and sectarian communities, and our military involvement there resulted from an ad hoc response to faulty intelligence in the aftermath of the 9-11 attacks. The first lesson we learned after toppling Saddam Hussein was that our main reason for invading the country—Iraq's nuclear-weapons program—didn't exist. We soon determined that another big reason for going, the supposed presence of Al Qaeda elements, was largely imaginary. But the really big and enduring lesson was that the Iraqis were not by nature a peaceful people. They had longstanding scores to settle, not only with each other but also with us, and they proved remarkably persistent in pursuing that purpose. If anything, our presence helped spur recruiting by sectarian militias [opposing military factions] and local supporters of al Qaeda.[44]

The Rise of AQI

Thompson's point about long-standing opposition between local Iraqi political and military factions is essential in understanding how ISIS eventually arose. Those conflicting groups were somewhat divided on political and social issues, but their most serious differences were religious in nature. As had been the case throughout the Middle East for many centuries, Iraqi Sunnis and Shias harbored deep-seated disagreements and hatreds. Because the dictator, Saddam Hussein, was a Sunni, his party enjoyed political and social dominance for decades, and Shia Iraqis had little or no say in how the country was run.

Meanwhile, the iron fist of Saddam Hussein's rule, enforced by his secret police, kept the influence of terrorists and other trouble-makers at a minimum. Despite this, al Qaeda had done its best to create a branch in Iraq in 1999. It went through a number of leaders and name changes in its infancy, but the West eventually referred to it as al Qaeda in Iraq (AQI). At first, the group encountered difficulties in organizing and accomplishing anything of note, in part because Saddam Hussein suppressed it. Despite his Sunni background, he ruled largely in a secular (nonreligious) manner, and al Qaeda viewed secular Muslim leaders as enemies. Hence, Saddam Hussein saw al Qaeda's attempts to infiltrate his country as a threat to his regime.

Only after US forces removed Saddam Hussein from power in 2003 was AQI able to make any serious headway. The following year, with the country in chaos in the wake of the US invasion, a Jordanian militant extremist named Abu Musab al-Zarqawi reestablished AQI. He and his chief AQI followers then launched an insurgency against the American forces occupying the country. That revolt was characterized by numerous acts of violence, among them suicide bombings and the kidnapping and execution of both Iraqi and Western hostages.

This new Iraqi chapter of al Qaeda, established amid the turmoil of the War on Terror, was destined to become the seed from which ISIS would ultimately grow. Creating a militant organization separate from al Qaeda was at the time not al-Zarqawi's intention, however. His principal goal was to increase AQI's size, reach, and power both in Iraq and the Middle East as a whole.

Sunni Discontent and Anger

The US occupation of Iraq played directly into al-Zarqawi's hands. After removing Saddam Hussein from power, American officials decided it would be dangerous to leave the dictator's military and police forces intact. US and British thinking was that these mostly Sunni fighters—under the leadership of some local wannabe strongman— might form a new army and attack the allied occupiers.

So American and British officials disbanded the former Iraqi military and police. Leaders of the occupation also got rid of various Iraqi

Saddam Hussein was held in power by conservative Sunni Muslims who filled many important government and industrial positions. When the United States and its allies deposed him, they stripped these officials of power, causing both unemployment and resentment among Sunni factions.

administrative and industrial positions that had long been filled by Sunnis appointed by Saddam Hussein. The overall US and British plan was to eliminate possible Saddam Hussein loyalists and start a new democratic country, including its government, from scratch. Moreover, and importantly, that new nation was slated to be run, almost by default, by Shias, who in the past had been oppressed by the Sunnis.

These moves proved to be almost as grave an error as the invasion itself had been. According to Harvard University scholar Garikai Chengu,

America, rather unwisely, destroyed Saddam Hussein's secular state machinery and replaced it with a predominantly Shia administration. The U.S. occupation caused vast unemployment in Sunni areas, by rejecting socialism and closing down factories in the naive hope that the magical hand of the free market would create jobs. Under the new U.S.-backed Shia regime, working class Sunnis lost hundreds of thousands of jobs. [Many] upper class Sunnis were systematically dispossessed of their assets and lost their political influence.[45]

Instead of promoting social and religious unity, therefore, US Iraqi policy worsened the traditional sectarian divisions and created a fertile breeding ground for Sunni discontent. Thousands of disgruntled former Sunni soldiers, policemen, administrators, and factory workers had little or no work. They could no longer support their families and as a result grew increasingly angry. Gradually, large numbers of them joined the insurgency that opposed the Western occupation. In this way, the War on Terror had inadvertently created the potential for more terrorism.

> "America, rather unwisely, destroyed Saddam Hussein's secular state machinery and replaced it with a predominantly Shia administration."[45]
>
> —Harvard University scholar Garikai Chengu

The insurrection in Iraq was at first not very well organized. It consisted of several small groups of insurgents, each of which had its personal gripes with the United States and its allies. As AQI itself became better organized, however, it formed a secret umbrella organization that helped to coordinate the plans and operations of the various Sunni insurgent groups.

Guided by al-Zarqawi and his lieutenants, members of these groups carried out terrorist attacks throughout Iraq. Not surprisingly, they made a point of targeting Americans and other Westerners. As a result, President Bush felt the need to further expand the War on Terror that he had initiated following 9/11 by sending more troops to Iraq. In response, the Iraqi-based terrorists struck out at Shia neighborhoods, stores, mosques, and markets. Massive bomb blasts rocked the capital, Baghdad, and other Iraqi cities on a regular basis, and thousands of civilians died each year. In 2008 alone, the estimated death toll was close to seven thousand, with many others wounded.

The Creation of the Caliphate

In the years that followed, the now greatly expanded AQI kept up its pressure on the Shia-controlled Iraqi government. Whenever possible,

A Recruitment Device for al Qaeda

The present consensus of terrorism experts is that ISIS formed in large part because of mistakes made during and after the US invasion of Iraq in 2003. Furthermore, they say, the invasion proved an unnecessary distraction from the ongoing War on Terror. Antiterrorism expert Richard A. Clarke, for example, contends that the advisers of President George W. Bush, who ordered the attack on Iraq, did not properly warn him of the dire consequences that might ensue from such an approach. "I doubt," Clarke writes, "that anyone ever had the chance to make the case to him that attacking Iraq would actually make America less secure and strengthen the broader radical Islamic terrorist movement." Clarke goes on,

> Any leader whom one can imagine as President on September 11 would have declared a "war on terrorism." [But] exactly what did George Bush do after September 11 that any other President one can imagine *wouldn't* have done after such attacks? In the end, what was unique about George Bush's reaction to terrorism was his selection as an object lesson for potential state sponsors of terrorism, not a country that had been engaging in anti-U.S. terrorism but one that had not been—Iraq. [Nothing] America could have done would have provided al Qaeda and its new generation of cloned groups a better recruitment device than our unprovoked invasion of an oil-rich Arab country.

Richard A. Clarke, *Against All Enemies: Inside America's War on Terror.* New York: Free Press, 2008, pp. 244, 246.

the emboldened terrorist group also attacked American, British, and other Western soldiers still stationed in the country. AQI then received another unexpected boost in 2011. That was the year of the so-called Arab Spring, consisting of a series of democratic uprisings in predominantly Arab nations, including Tunisia, Egypt, and Libya.

Another country rocked by the Arab Spring was Syria, lying along Iraq's western border. Syrian dictator Bashar al-Assad felt threatened by the many local demonstrators who called on him and his government to institute democratic reforms. He reacted to these demands by arresting thousands of protestors and sending army tanks into various Syrian cities.

Soon Syria was in a state of civil war, and AQI saw the chaos there as an opportunity for it to expand its influence across the border. New branches of the terrorist group sprang up in Syria in 2012 and 2013. Meanwhile, more disaffected Sunni Iraqis joined the group's ranks. As the organization grew, its leaders adopted even bigger goals. In June 2014 those leaders decided to transform the group into a caliphate—a medieval term for a large-scale Islamic kingdom or empire. The objective became to expand the group's control around the world and, where necessary, use force to absorb entire peoples and nations.

Given the group's new and audacious global aims, its leaders felt it was no longer appropriate to call it AQI. They therefore changed its name to the Islamic State of Iraq and Syria, or ISIS. The freshly

The aftermath of a bomb explosion in Aleppo, Syria, reveals the level of destruction experienced by civilians caught up in the fight among the Syrian military, antigovernment forces, and ISIS. The latter has brought in many militants from Iraq and nearby countries to destabilize the region.

christened organization had, by a series of twists and turns, developed over the course of more than a dozen years. The War on Terror had created widespread chaos in the Middle East, especially in Iraq, which had provided fertile ground for a group like ISIS to grow.

Once established, ISIS began to flex its proverbial muscles. Gangs of ISIS members drove into villages in eastern Syria and western Iraq and used threats and sometimes murder to intimidate local populations into doing what they were told. In this way the caliphate, in a sense thumbing its nose at the West's ongoing antiterrorism efforts, rapidly grew until it controlled hundreds of square miles of territory. Its soldiers even managed to take over some bustling cities, including Raqqa in Syria and Mosul in Iraq. (Raqqa became the group's official headquarters.)

To keep these operations rolling and its members under control and loyal, ISIS needed a steady flow of money. Some of it, particularly at first, was stolen from bank vaults in the newly acquired territories. Moreover, as explained by Tewfik Cassis, a correspondent for the news journal the *Week*, ISIS's leaders came to employ additional means of gaining funding:

> Before ISIS formally controlled Mosul, it would run a racketeering business (similar to that used by the U.S. mafia) under the nose of the Iraqi government. Businesses and individuals had to pay them a "protection fee" to stay safe. Properties belonging to religious minorities or Iraqi regime sympathizers were promptly appropriated (for example churches, gold, hard currency), and once ISIS controlled territory and people it began taxing them like any state would. It is the Middle East, so oil is always involved. While technically shut out from the international markets, ISIS could and did still find illegal markets for its oil.[46]

The Survival of ISIS

ISIS also daringly planned or inspired terrorist attacks in Western countries, including France, Denmark, Australia, and the United States. In addition, Westerners and non-Westerners alike were targeted in predominantly Muslim nations, among them Turkey, Tunisia, Egypt, and Yemen. By December 2016 the group was responsible for more than a thousand deaths outside of Iraq and Syria.

As ISIS has grown bolder, Iraqi and Western leaders have tried to minimize its threat. For example, in 2007 US, French, and other allied air strikes and ground attacks by Iraqi troops hammered ISIS positions, which kept the Islamic State from further territorial expansion. Despite this success, some antiterrorism experts worry that it might take many years to completely eradicate ISIS.

Though experts debate how long the brutal terrorist organization will survive, the manner in which ISIS formed is not in question. University of San Francisco scholar Stephen Zunes articulates this consensus opinion. "The rise of ISIS is a direct consequence of the U.S. invasion and occupation of Iraq," he asserts. "While there are a number of other contributing factors as well, that fateful decision is paramount." Had the United States not decided to invade Iraq as part of its War on Terror, Zunes points out, "the reign of terror ISIS has imposed upon large swathes of Syria and Iraq" would "never have happened."[47]

> "Before ISIS formally controlled Mosul, it would run a racketeering business (similar to that used by the U.S. mafia) under the nose of the Iraqi government."[46]
>
> —Journalist Tewfik Cassis

CHAPTER FIVE

How Has the War on Terror Altered Global Terrorism?

Focus Questions

1. Why might President George W. Bush have used the term *war on terror* rather than *management of terror* or some other term that might have been more accurate?
2. In your view, can the War on Terror be called a success if terrorist attacks have increased in areas outside the United States? Why or why not?
3. Do you think that instilling fear in people can work to further an individual's or organization's aims? Why or why not?

There is no doubt in the minds of Western counterterrorism experts that the War on Terror has altered global terrorism. However, experts frequently disagree about whether the War on Terror has been successful overall, or even in part. The nonprofit international watchdog organization Saferworld sums up this at times bewildering lack of accord, saying,

> Western governments have placed responding to "terrorism," "violent extremism" and instability among their foremost priorities. They have led international military interventions into Iraq and Afghanistan, targeted militant groups directly in Somalia, Yemen, Pakistan, and elsewhere, and provided significant support to regional allies to confront these threats to international security and build more stable states. Yet, despite the investment of huge resources—human, financial, military and political—the results of these actions have been mixed.[48]

This idea that the War on Terror has had mixed success is borne out by differences of opinion among various authorities on terrorism and antiterrorist efforts. Some say the West is winning the conflict against terrorists. Others hold that the West is losing, or at least cannot win, that ongoing battle. Similarly, death tolls due to terrorism and other statistics related to the War on Terror can often be interpreted in conflicting ways. Much of this confusion seems to stem from the very natures of terrorism and counterterrorism. As Brookings Institution foreign relations expert Daniel L. Byman points out, "Successful counter-terrorism is difficult to measure. Unlike a conventional military campaign, there is no enemy capital to capture, or army or industrial base to destroy. Even a terrorist organization that is divided and demoralized still has the capability to lash out and kill many innocents."[49]

> "Successful counter-terrorism is difficult to measure."[49]
>
> —Foreign relations expert Daniel L. Byman

Can the War Be Won?

Thus, although the War on Terror has altered global terrorism, it is sometimes difficult to say whether its effects have been positive or negative. The ongoing argument among the experts over which side's strategies have been most effective is a clear example. Many of those experts tout the success of Western nations. They point out that the world did not undergo the catastrophic changes that al Qaeda and other terrorist groups had initially hoped for.

After pulling off the 9/11 attacks, for instance, Osama bin Laden and his followers were sure they could dramatically weaken the United States in only a few years. But that did not happen. Al Qaeda and other terrorist groups had underestimated the determination of the American people, and Westerners in general, to fight for their way of life. The Western nations rebounded from 9/11, launched the War on Terror, and took the fight to the terrorists' own homelands.

Other experts argue that just as the terrorists failed to appreciate the resolve of their enemies, so too did Western countries initially underestimate the determination and resilience of the terrorists. The fact that terrorists continue to operate worldwide, they say, calls into question the wisdom of calling American antiterrorism efforts a war

Despite billions of dollars spent and many lives lost in the struggle, the War on Terror has produced mixed results. For example, America ended military action in Afghanistan in 2014, but since then the Taliban has reemerged, and US troops still stationed there have come under attack.

on terror. Most Americans view a war as something a country either wins or loses, these experts point out. So when the American people heard that they were engaged in a war against terrorism, the general assumption was that sooner or later there would be a clear-cut victory.

But as political scientist Philip H. Gordon puts it, achieving a victory over an abstract concept such as terrorism is not realistic. "What does victory—or defeat—mean in a war on terror?" he asks. "Will this kind of war ever end? How long will it take? Would we see victory coming? Would we recognize it when it came?"[50] Military analyst Andrew Bacevich answers these questions, saying, "We cannot eradicate terrorism any more than we can eradicate armed robbery. The best we can hope for is to reduce it to tolerable proportions."[51] Richard Haass, the noted former chairman of the Council on Foreign Relations, agrees. "Eliminating or eradicating the threat is impossible," he states. "We could be 99.99% effective and there would still be enough people to cause real harm. The goal should be to reduce—dramatically—the scale of the threat and what it [terrorism] can accomplish."[52]

For these reasons, Bacevich, Haass, and many other experts disliked using the term *War on Terror* from the start. They were relieved when President Obama and other Western leaders replaced it with *Overseas Contingency Operations* in 2013. (Nevertheless, many people still informally call it the War on Terror.) Whatever one may call this ongoing conflict against terrorist organizations, it can be won, Gordon stresses. But it will not happen in the conventional sense—that is, by bombing and killing all existing terrorists. Even if one could eradicate every living terrorist, he writes, newly radicalized individuals would take their places. Victory will come, he says,

> "The goal should be to reduce— dramatically— the scale of the threat and what it [terrorism] can accomplish."[52]
>
> —Richard Haass, former chairman of the Council on Foreign Relations

> when political changes erode and ultimately undermine support for the ideology and strategy of those determined to destroy the United States. It will come not when Washington and its allies kill or capture all terrorists or potential terrorists, but when the ideology the terrorists espouse is discredited, when their tactics are seen to have failed, and when they come to find more promising paths to the dignity, respect, and opportunities they crave.[53]

Grandiose Dreams of World Domination

In the face of disagreements over whether the War on Terror will or even can be won, some government officials, antiterrorism experts, and

Hard to Measure Success

Noted political commentator Brian Michael Jenkins here explains some of the reasons why progress in the War on Terror is often slow and hard to measure, and why people often believe the war is being lost though facts suggest otherwise.

> Progress is difficult to assess in this type of contest. There are no obvious metrics [methods of measuring gains and losses]. Terrorist attacks are designed to be dramatic events, calculated to capture attention and create alarm, which will cause people to exaggerate the strength of the terrorists and the threat they pose. The public sees every terrorist attack as a failure, a battle lost. Moreover, progress in degrading terrorists' operational capabilities, slowing terrorist recruiting, or impeding terrorists' financing seems slow, is not easily portrayed, and remains emotionally unsatisfying in the face of terrorist outrages. [Every] terrorist attack is seen as proof that counter-terrorism efforts are not working. Credibility is another problem. Premature claims by U.S. officials that suggest the mission has been accomplished or that the United States is within reach of defeating al-Qaeda have eroded government credibility. And in today's highly partisan political environment, every attack is portrayed as evidence that the administration is incompetent, negligent, or worse. Every claim of progress is challenged. The political debate contributes to the atmosphere of fear.

Brian Michael Jenkins, "Fifteen Years On, Where Are We in the 'War on Terror'?," Combating Terrorism Center, September 7, 2016. www.ctc.usma.edu.

leading journalists call for striving for some sort of middle ground. Former *Newsweek* reporters Sam Stein and Jessica Schulberg, for instance, state that "the United States will—for the foreseeable future and likely beyond—be forced to *manage* the threat of terrorism rather than get rid of it."[54]

In fact, Stein, Schulberg, and others hold that the United States and its allies more or less employed this management approach as a chief strategy between 2001 and 2017. Furthermore, they argue, it was by and large successful. The evidence for that success, in this view, is that during those years no terrorist organization was able to achieve its primary goals.

The chief aims that Bin Laden stated for al Qaeda just after 9/11 are a clear example. The "evil" US government would be the first Western "autocratic regime" to fall, he predicted. The governments of Britain and other US allies would soon follow. "Once the autocratic regimes responsible for the humiliation of the Muslim world have been removed," Bin Laden said, "it will be possible to return it to the idealized state of Arabia at the time of the Prophet Muhammad. A caliphate will be established from Morocco to Central Asia, [strict Islamic] rule will prevail, Israel will be destroyed, oil prices will skyrocket, and the United States will recoil in humiliation and possibly even collapse."[55]

At the time, large numbers of Americans and other Westerners worried that al Qaeda might be capable of achieving at least some of these ambitions in the years ahead. Not long after 9/11, Richard A. Clarke points out, al Qaeda was routinely viewed as "a worldwide political conspiracy." Its objective seemed to be to create "a fourteenth-century-style theocracy in which women have no rights [and] everyone is forced to be a Muslim." Al Qaeda clearly wanted to bring about "the destruction of the United States," Clarke says, and was widely seen as "our number one enemy."[56]

Many Westerners took al Qaeda's rhetoric to heart. In particular, large numbers of Americans believed that more attacks on the enormous scale of 9/11 might occur at any moment. Time has shown, however, that both al Qaeda's grandiose dreams of world domination and most Westerners' estimation of that group's capabilities were overblown. As it turned out, no terrorist attack on the scale of 9/11 has occurred. "By 2016," Brian Michael Jenkins points out, "America's terrorist foes had not been able to launch another 9/11-scale attack— they had not even come close."[57] Before 9/11, the United States had been unprepared for an assault of that kind, Jenkins says. Immediately afterward, however, US leaders and their allies launched the War on

"By 2016, America's terrorist foes had not been able to launch another 9/11-scale attack— they had not even come close."[57]

—Counterterrorism expert Brian Michael Jenkins

Terror, which, he states, has helped nations prepare for and prevent such attacks.

Those who contend that the West's management and containment strategy has largely worked say that that success can be seen in the relatively small number of people killed by terrorists after 9/11. Jenkins, for example, points to statistics that show how the War on Terror kept the global impact of al Qaeda and other terrorist groups far smaller than the terrorists would have liked. He writes, "Jihadist terrorists since 9/11 have managed to kill fewer than 100 people in the United States." These were "all needless tragedies to be sure. But an average of six or seven jihadist-inspired murders a year in a country with an annual average of 14,000 to 15,000 homicides is a far better outcome than many people had feared in 2001."[58]

Other observers point out that between 2001 and 2017 the chances of a US resident being killed on American soil by a foreign terrorist were small. "In the United States," according to the political watchdog publication *Washington Monthly*,

> the terrorism threat is even smaller than it is in the West generally. With the exception of the huge Sept. 11 and Oklahoma City attacks, there is no year since 1970 when terrorism killed more than 50 people in the United States. [In 2015] the number was 44, according to the Global Terrorism Database. That means that terrorism typically kills about as many Americans as lightning strikes do.[59]

Domestic Lone Wolves

Though the War on Terror appears to have made the United States safer from foreign terrorists, terrorist attacks do still occur in the nation. The principal terrorist threat today, many experts say, is homegrown in nature. Antiterrorism authorities often call domestic perpetrators of terror lone wolves. Studies of domestic terrorist attacks that have occurred indicate that most of the killers were not inspired by al Qaeda or ISIS, as many Americans may have assumed. Although a few of the lone wolves were roused to action by foreign extremist groups, most were local right-wing nationalists and white supremacist types angry about US political and social trends. According to *Newsweek* journalist Kurt Eichenwald, American-born right-wing militants

> have killed more people in the United States than jihadis have. [These] Americans thrive on hate and conspiracy theories, many fed to them by politicians and commentators who blithely blather about government concentration camps and impending martial law and plans to seize guns and other dystopian gibberish, apparently unaware there are people listening who don't know it's all lies. These extremists turn to violence—against minorities, non-Christians, abortion providers, government officials—in what they believe is a fight to save America.[60]

The terrorists in question were Americans motivated by a number of varied grievances. Both supporters and critics of the War on Terror agree that eliminating all such homegrown threats is next to impossible. It is extremely difficult, they say, to predict if and when an American will suddenly become a terrorist and strike out at his or her own country. The continuing reality of domestic terrorist attacks makes deciding whether the War on Terror has been successful even more difficult.

"[American-born right-wing militants] have killed more people in the United States than jihadis have."[60]

—*Newsweek* journalist Kurt Eichenwald

Terrorist Successes in Non-Western Nations

Many experts argue that pointing only to the frequency of terrorist attacks in the United States to gauge the success of the War on Terror is misleading. Although there were no other large-scale terrorist attacks in the United States after 9/11, they point out, a number of such attacks did occur during the post-9/11 years. The difference was that those incidents happened in other parts of the world. For instance, western Europe experienced far more terrorist incidents and suffered nineteen times more deaths at terrorists' hands than the United States did in those years.

A car bomb detonated outside a stadium in Gombe, Nigeria, where that nation's president was attending a rally. The explosion killed the bomber and injured eighteen others. Nigeria is just one of several nations experiencing higher levels of terrorist activities since the War on Terror began.

Even worse off were the five nations where the vast majority of terrorist incidents occur each year. They are Iraq, Afghanistan, Pakistan, and Syria, all in the Middle East, and Nigeria in western Africa. In 2014, for instance, 78 percent of all the people killed by terrorists lived in those five countries. One major reason why the four Middle Eastern nations have been hit so often is that the headquarters of ISIS and several of al Qaeda's offshoots lie within their borders.

Nigeria, meanwhile, witnessed the biggest increase in terrorist deaths ever recorded by any country. By 2015, annual deaths there caused by terrorist incidents had swelled by more than 300 percent, reaching 7,512 that year. There is no mystery about why this has happened, antiterrorism experts say. Presently the world's deadliest terrorist group, Boko Haram—inspired by and allied with ISIS—operates primarily in Nigeria.

Some authorities on terrorism and counterterrorism argue that there is a serious downside to this redistribution of terrorist organizations like Boko Haram to that handful of countries. Namely, these nations are much smaller and economically and militarily weaker than the United States. Terrorist groups have more ability to operate freely

Destined for the Ash Heap of History

Widely respected political scientist Philip H. Gordon holds that the West will inevitably win the war against terrorists. But it will take time, he asserts, and will happen only when the terrorists' arguments appear unappealing to all but a tiny handful of misguided individuals.

The risk of terrorism in the United States could be reduced if officials reallocated hundreds of billions of dollars per year in domestic spending to homeland security measures, significantly curtailed civil liberties to ensure that no potential terrorists were on the streets, and invaded and occupied countries that might one day support or sponsor terrorism. Pursuing that goal in this way, however, would have costs that would vastly outweigh the benefits of reaching the goal, even if reaching it were possible. [The] war on terror will end with the collapse of the violent ideology that caused it—when al Qaeda's cause comes to be seen by its potential adherents as a failure, when they turn against it and adopt other goals and other means. Communism, too, once seemed vibrant and attractive to millions around the world, but over time it came to be seen as a failure. [Like] communism today, extremist Islam in the future will have a few adherents here and there. But as an organized ideology capable of taking over states or inspiring large numbers of people, it will have been effectively dismantled, discredited, and discarded. And [Osama] bin Laden's violent ideology will end up on the ash heap of history.

Philip H. Gordon, "Can the War on Terror Be Won?," Brookings Institution, November 1, 2007. www.brookings.edu.

in such weaker nations. Therefore, critics of the War on Terror say, terrorists have stepped up their attacks inside those countries, leading to more terrorism worldwide. In 2014, for example, the total number of global deaths from terrorism was 80 percent higher than in 2013. Also, the yearly number of terrorism-related deaths worldwide rose from 7,473 in 2011 to 32,685 in 2014.

Sidetracked in Iraq?

Another frequent critique of the War on Terror makes the point that at times major aspects of the US and Western antiterrorism strategy proved unwise and ill conceived. On the positive side, they admit, efforts to track down terrorist leaders and to disrupt al Qaeda and its global offshoots were often thoughtful and effective. Such positive efforts clearly dominated the conflict in the months immediately following 9/11.

However, the critics continue, the architects of the War on Terror allowed themselves to be sidetracked, especially in Iraq, beginning in 2003. After September 11, Clarke asserts,

> one would have thought [that] high on the priority list would have been improving U.S. relations with the Islamic world, in order to dry up support for the deviant variant of Islam that is al Qaeda. After all, al Qaeda, the enemy that attacked us, was engaged in its own highly successful propaganda campaign to influence millions of Muslims to act against America. [But] far from addressing the popular appeal of the enemy that attacked us, [President] Bush handed that enemy precisely what it wanted and needed, proof that America was at war with Islam, that we were the new Crusaders come to occupy Muslim land.[61]

The ill-considered Iraq invasion did more than bolster al Qaeda's propaganda efforts, the critics say. It also diverted intelligence and military resources worth billions of dollars from the War on Terror to the removal of Saddam Hussein and the suppression of the subsequent Iraqi insurgency. Moreover, that uprising eventually produced another dangerous terrorist organization—ISIS.

US soldiers in Iraq walk with an Iraqi mother and her children. The presence of US soldiers in Islamic nations has given terrorists fuel to spark more anti-American sentiment. Many troops find it difficult to operate in these regions because it can be hard to tell friends from enemies and civilians from combatants.

Personal Defiance Against Terrorism

None of the experts—whether they see the War on Terror as largely a success or mostly a failure—believes that America has become immune to the efforts of terrorists. There is general agreement that US counterterrorism forces must remain always vigilant to ensure that plots by such extremists fail.

Many experts point out that regardless of the perceived success or failure of government counterterrorism activities, one thing is certain: terrorists are successful when they make people feel terrorized. And one thing that ISIS extremists and other terrorists have been effective at, the experts concede, is scaring people. That, after all, is the chief motive of terrorism in the first place. Gordon, Haass, and Clarke are among the many experts who say that Americans in particular too often fall for terrorist propaganda. They also listen too frequently to doomsaying politicians who see foreign terrorists behind every bush. That alarmist point of view, Clarke has repeatedly said, only gives the terrorists credit for strengths and abilities they do not actually possess.

To do their part in fighting against international terrorism, Gordon advises, Americans should "not overreact to threats" from foreign terrorists. They should instead "demonstrate confidence in the country's values and its society—and the determination to preserve both." Americans, Gordon says, will sleep easier if they adhere to a personal, as well as national, policy "of defiantly refusing to allow terrorists to change [their] way of life." That, he adds, will give every US citizen "good reason to be confident that in the long run they will prevail."[62]

Introduction: Not the First American War on Terror

1. George W. Bush, "Address to Congress and the American People Following the Sept. 11, 2001 Attacks." www.history2u.com.
2. Thomas Jefferson, *The Life and Writings of Thomas Jefferson*, ed. S.E. Forman. Whitefish, MT: Kessinger, 2007, p. 215.
3. Robert F. Turner, "State Responsibility and the War on Terror: The Legacy of Thomas Jefferson and the Barbary Pirates," *Chicago Journal of International Law*, vol. 4, April 2003, p. 137.
4. Turner, "State Responsibility and the War on Terror," pp. 137–39.

Chapter One: A Brief History of the War on Terror

5. Barack Obama, "Remarks by the President at the National Defense University, May 23, 2013," Obama White House. https://obamawhitehouse.archives.gov.
6. Osama bin Laden, "Jihad Against Jews and Crusaders: World Islamic Front Statement," Federation of American Scientists. https://fas.org.
7. Bush, "Address to Congress and the American People Following the Sept. 11, 2001 Attacks."
8. Bush, "Address to Congress and the American People Following the Sept. 11, 2001 Attacks."
9. George W. Bush, "National Strategy for Combating Terrorism," Bush White House, February 14, 2003. https://georgewbush-whitehouse.archives.gov.
10. Heritage Foundation, "Terrorism." http://solutions.heritage.org.
11. Rand Corporation, "Terrorism Threat Assessment." www.rand.org.

Chapter Two: How Did the 9/11 Attacks Launch the War on Terror?

12. George J. Tenet, "Director Tenet's Statement to CIA Workforce About Terrorist Attacks," September 12, 2001. www.cia.gov.
13. Tenet, "Director Tenet's Statement to CIA Workforce About Terrorist Attacks."
14. Quoted in ABC News, "Calm Before the Crash," 9-11 Research. http://911research.wtc7.net.

15. Wesley B. Truitt, *Power and Policy: Lessons for Leaders in Government and Business.* Santa Barbara, CA: ABC-CLIO, 2010, p. 104.
16. George W. Bush, "Statement by the President in His Address to the Nation, September 11, 2001," Bush White House. https://georgewbush-whitehouse.archives.gov.
17. Bush, "Statement by the President in His Address to the Nation, September 11, 2001."
18. George W. Bush, "Remarks by the President in Photo Opportunity with the National Security Team, September 12, 2001," Bush White House. https://georgewbush-whitehouse.archives.gov.
19. Congress.gov, "Congressional Bill S.J.Res.23: Authorization for Use of Military Force, September 14, 2001." www.congress.gov.
20. Congress.gov, "Congressional Bill S.J.Res.23."
21. Quoted in Rachael Smolkin, "Congress Moves Swiftly to Back Action by Bush," *Pittsburgh Post-Gazette*, September 15, 2001. www.post-gazette.com.
22. Quoted in Smolkin, "Congress Moves Swiftly to Back Action by Bush."
23. Quoted in *Guardian*, "Bush Rejects Taliban Offer to Hand Bin Laden Over," October 14, 2001. www.theguardian.com.
24. Bush, "Remarks by the President in Photo Opportunity with the National Security Team, September 12, 2001."
25. Bush, "Remarks by the President in Photo Opportunity with the National Security Team, September 12, 2001."

Chapter Three: How Did the Killing of Osama bin Laden Weaken al Qaeda?

26. Richard A. Clarke, *Against All Enemies: Inside America's War on Terror.* New York: Free Press, 2008, p. 287.
27. Quoted in Gordon Corera, "Bin Laden's Tora Bora Escape, Just Months After 9/11," BBC News, July 11, 2011. www.bbc.com.
28. Quoted in Corera, "Bin Laden's Tora Bora Escape, Just Months After 9/11."
29. Quoted in Wayne Parry, "NJ 9/11 Widow Can't Forgive Bin Laden," *Deseret News*, May 2, 2011. www.deseretnews.com.
30. Quoted in Tori DeAngelis, "Bin Laden's Death: What Does It Mean? Political and Social Psychologists Weigh In," American Psychological Association. www.apa.org.

31. Quoted in James Kitfield, "How the Killing of Bin Laden Has Crippled al Qaeda," *Atlantic,* April 30, 2012. www.theatlantic.com.

32. Quoted in Kitfield, "How the Killing of Bin Laden Has Crippled al Qaeda."

33. Quoted in DeAngelis, "Bin Laden's Death."

34. Quoted in DeAngelis, "Bin Laden's Death."

35. Brian Michael Jenkins, "Five Years After the Death of Osama bin Laden, Is the World Safer?," *Rand Blog,* May 2, 2016. www.rand.org.

36. Kitfield, "How the Killing of Bin Laden Has Crippled al Qaeda."

37. Kitfield, "How the Killing of Bin Laden Has Crippled al Qaeda."

38. Jenkins, "Five Years After the Death of Osama bin Laden, Is the World Safer?"

39. Quoted in Kitfield, "How the Killing of Bin Laden Has Crippled al Qaeda."

40. Jenkins, "Five Years After the Death of Osama bin Laden, Is the World Safer?"

41. Jenkins, "Five Years After the Death of Osama bin Laden, Is the World Safer?"

Chapter Four: How Did the War on Terror Contribute to the Founding of ISIS?

42. John Badahur Lamb, "The Enduring Damage of 9/11: How the War on Terror Gave Rise to a Bigger Threat in the Form of ISIS," *Salon,* September 11, 2016. www.salon.com.

43. Quoted in *Washington Post*, "President Bush Delivers Remarks on the War on Terrorism, December 12, 2005." www.washingtonpost.com.

44. Loren Thompson, "Iraq: The Biggest Mistake in American Military History," *Forbes,* December 15, 2011. www.forbes.com.

45. Garikai Chengu, "How the U.S. Helped Create Al Qaeda and ISIS," *CounterPunch Magazine,* September 19, 2014. www.counterpunch.org.

46. Tewfik Cassis, "A Brief History of ISIS," *Week,* November 21, 2015. http://theweek.com.

47. Stephen Zunes, "The US and the Rise of ISIS," Common Dreams, December 10, 2015. www.commondreams.org.

Chapter Five: How Has the War on Terror Altered Global Terrorism?

48. Saferworld, "Constructive Alternatives to Counter-Terror and Stabilisation." www.saferworld.org.uk.
49. Daniel L. Byman, "Are We Winning the War on Terrorism?," Brookings Institution, May 23, 2003. www.brookings.edu.
50. Philip H. Gordon, "Can the War on Terror Be Won?," Brookings Institution, November 1, 2007. www.brookings.edu.
51. Quoted in Sam Stein and Jessica Schulberg, "We Aren't Going to Eradicate ISIS, Now or Anytime Soon," *Huffington Post,* December 19, 2016. www.huffingtonpost.com.
52. Quoted in Stein and Schulberg, "We Aren't Going to Eradicate ISIS, Now or Anytime Soon."
53. Gordon, "Can the War on Terror Be Won?"
54. Stein and Schulberg, "We Aren't Going to Eradicate ISIS, Now or Anytime Soon."
55. Quoted in Gordon, "Can the War on Terror Be Won?"
56. Clarke, *Against All Enemies,* p. 218.
57. Jenkins, "Five Years After the Death of Osama bin Laden, Is the World Safer?"
58. Jenkins, "Five Years After the Death of Osama bin Laden, Is the World Safer?"
59. Nancy LeTourneau, "A Reality Check on the Threat of Terrorism," *Washington Monthly*, August 17, 2016. http://washingtonmonthly.com.
60. Kurt Eichenwald, "Right Wing Extremists Are a Bigger Threat to America than ISIS," *Newsweek,* February 4, 2016. www.newsweek.com.
61. Clarke, *Against All Enemies,* pp. 245–46.
62. Gordon, "Can the War on Terror Be Won?"

Books

Noah Berlastky, *The War on Terror*. Farmington Hills, MI: Greenhaven, 2012.

Matthew Heines, *American Experiences in Arabia During the War on Terror*. Charleston, SC: Amazon Digital Services, 2015.

Brendan January, *ISIS: The Global Face of Terrorism*. Minneapolis: Twenty-First Century, 2017.

David Keiran et al., *The War of My Generation: Youth Culture and the War on Terror*. New Brunswick, NJ: Rutgers University Press, 2015.

Elaine Landau, *Osama bin Laden: The Life and Death of the 9/11 al-Qaeda Mastermind*. Minneapolis: Twenty-First Century, 2013.

Elizabeth Schmermund, *Domestic Terrorism*. Farmington Hills, MI: Greenhaven, 2017.

David Smethurst, *Tripoli: The United States' First War on Terror*. Charleston, SC: Amazon Digital Services, 2016.

Internet Sources

Steven Bucci, James Carafano, and Jessica Zuckerman, *Fifty Terror Plots Foiled Since 9/11: The Homegrown Threat and the Long War on Terrorism*, Heritage Foundation, April 25, 2012. www.heritage.org/terrorism/report/fifty-terror-plots-foiled-911-the-homegrown-threat-and-the-long-war-terrorism.

George W. Bush, "National Strategy for Combating Terrorism," Bush White House, February 14, 2003. https://georgewbush-whitehouse.archives.gov/news/releases/2003/02/20030214-7.html.

Tewfik Cassis, "A Brief History of ISIS," *Week,* November 21, 2015. http://theweek.com/articles/589924/brief-history-isis.

Philip H. Gordon, "Can the War on Terror Be Won?," Brookings Institution, November 1, 2007. www.brookings.edu/wp-content/uploads/2016/06/11terrorism.pdf.

Christopher Hitchens, "Jefferson vs. the Muslim Pirates," *City Journal,* Spring 2007. www.city-journal.org/html/jefferson-versus-muslim
-pirates-13013.html.

Ryan Lizza, "ISIS, Terrorist Sanctuaries, and the Lessons of 9/11," *New Yorker,* November 19, 2015. www.newyorker.com/news/daily
-comment/isis-terrorist-sanctuaries-and-the-lessons-of-911.

John Maraia, "The Impact of Osama bin Laden's Death on al-Qaida," US Institute of Peace, May 2, 2011. www.usip.org/publications/the
-impact-osama-bin-ladens-death-al-qaida.

Websites

CBS News, "The Fight Against ISIS" (www.cbsnews.com/isis). This fulsome collection of articles about ISIS covers its formation and nearly all aspects of its terror attacks and Western efforts to thwart its progress.

Central Intelligence Agency, "The CIA and the War on Terror" (www.cia.gov/news-information/cia-the-war-on-terrorism/). The CIA created this highly useful timeline of the war on terror. Clicking on the highlighted dates takes the reader to all sorts of crucial documents, speeches, and other primary source documents.

Global Security.org, "Al-Qaida/Al-Qaeda (the Base)" (www.glo balsecurity.org/military/world/para/al-qaida.htm). This site contains a wide range of accurate information about the terrorist group al Qaeda, including its known affiliates and spin-off groups around the world.

Historian and award-winning writer Don Nardo has written numerous books about warfare in various ages and cultures. Among them are studies of weapons, strategies, tactics, battles, and national policies in ancient Mesopotamia, Egypt, Greece, and Rome; medieval Europe and Japan; the American Revolution; the American Indian wars; the American Civil War; World War II; the Persian Gulf War; and the War on Terror. Nardo lives with his wife, Christine, in Massachusetts.